THE MARRIAGE ABCs

UFUOMAEE

THE MARRIAGE ABCs

Copyright © 2021 Ufuomaee

Amazon Print Edition

All rights reserved.

ISBN: 9798546103996

This book was originally a series, published first on blog.ufuomaee.org from 2016 to 2017.

All rights reserved. No part of this publication may be reproduced, stored, or transmitted in any form or by any means, electronic, mechanical, photocopying, recording, scanning, or otherwise without written permission from the publisher. It is illegal to copy this book, post it to a website, or distribute it by any other means without permission.

This book is for a mature audience. Ufuomaee is not a trained marriage counsellor nor a therapist. The advice given here is just what it is; her advice based on an understanding of Scripture and the New Covenant for Christians. Whatever the situation, Ufuomaee does not condone nor excuse domestic violence nor spousal abuse.

Ufuomaee asserts the moral right to be identified as the author of this work.

Photo credit: www.canva.com

Cover design: business.ufuomaee.org

DEDICATION

To every sincere believer in Christ Jesus who wishes to have a happy marriage.
I dedicate this book to you so that, if you're single, you will enter with open eyes, and if you're already married, you might learn and practice wisdom in your marriage.
If you are going through a tough marriage, I pray that this book will enlighten, inspire, and motivate you to remain faithful and abide in Christ so that you may bear His fruit at the end of your pruning.
Amen.
To God be all the glory!

TABLE OF CONTENTS

Foreword	vii
Preface	ix
A for Appreciation	p1
B for Blessed to Bless	p8
C for Communicate Effectively	p18
D for Die Daily to Self	p27
E for Expectations, Expectation	p36
F for Friends Forever	p46
G for Grow in Grace	p50
H for Honesty is the Best Policy	p57
I for Intimacy	p62
J for JOY!	p70
K for Kiss and Keep Kissing	p74
L for L.O.V.E	p79
M for Money Matters	p87
N for Nobody's Perfect: Negotiate and Never Give Up	p93
O for Offspring	p97

P for Passion, Purpose and Prosperity	p103
Q for Quality over Quantity	p108
R for Respect is Reciprocal	p113
S for Sex and Sexuality (1)	p121
S for Sex and Sexuality (2)	p128
T for Temptation	p136
U for Unity	p143
V for Victory in the Vine	p148
W for Wisdom is the Principal Thing	p156
X for Xclusive!	p161
Y for Yield to Love	p165
Z for Zealous for Life	p168
Help! I Married a Wolf!	p173
Emotional Abuse – The Silent Killer	p183
Other Resources	p187
References	p188
Acknowledgments	p190
About the Author	p191

FOREWORD

BY PASTOR JOHN ONOJEHARHO

The Marriage ABCs is not as simple as 'ABC.' ABC is used to describe something that is usually simple, straight forward, and not complicated. However, The Marriage ABCs is a typical example of why we should not judge a book by its cover. The title, without circumspect, is deceptively a shallow 'ABC,' but the content is very profound and deep.

The Marriage ABCs will resonate differently with people according to their experiences, I dare say, inexperiences, and their fantasies regarding marriage. In one compendium, the author has, in one fell swoop, explained what marriage is, what marriage is not, and what marriage should be.

The Marriage ABCs is a collection of twenty-six books so ingeniously strung together by the author in one conversation regarding marriage: the good, the bad, and the ugly of this exclusively human enterprise. The sweet and the bitter too. The Marriage ABCs constantly reminds us of the role and supremacy of God in the marriage endeavour and how He turns up for us when we sail into stormy waters. He is indeed our ever-present help in times of trouble.

Though The Marriage ABCs is fundamentally Christian, its contents apply to all mankind and all religions. Apart from X for Xclusivity, the collection is religion-blind, and there is a lesson for everyone in each of the twenty-six letters that make up The Marriage ABCs.

There are no dull chapters in this book. I recommend it to all who are already in a marital relationship, all who are planning to enter into marriage, and all who opt to stay single.

PREFACE

You might be wondering; who are you? Are you married? Happily? How many years have you been married? What qualifies you to teach on this deep and sensitive matter? Are you not concerned that you might mislead others?

Deep breath. Wow.

Maybe you're not wondering that. I know I would care if I was reading a book about business from someone who has failed at business, or whose current business venture is failing. I would doubt that he or she knows what it really takes to build a successful business.

Truthfully, if I had let these questions hinder me from writing what God led me to write, through the challenges in my own marriage, then you wouldn't have **The Marriage ABCs**. Or maybe He would have used someone else more qualified in marriage to write a much better book. But the thing is, He used me.

Like you, I am a reader of my own works. I am one of the people I write for. I write, not from the position of accomplishment but the point of inspiration; as the Lord the ministers to me, I minister to others. In fact, I didn't write The Marriage ABCs for you. I wrote it for myself, for the most part. But you can also join me to read and learn the truths God has shared with me. Maybe it will help you in your marriage or relationship.

But to try to answer the foregoing questions; I am a child of God who is deeply flawed. I often struggle with being very opinionated, idealistic, and neurotic. Through my own life experience and walk with God, I have developed very strong convictions about my Faith and about life in general. You may see this as you read through this book.

I got married in May 2013. At the time I started the series, I was three years in and believed what I was experiencing in my marriage was common, typical, and could be overcome by simply being the best follower of Jesus Christ as I could be, living in obedience and trust. I wouldn't describe my marriage as happy, then or now. My marriage inspires some of my writing, and I am still on this journey with God, trusting and obeying while asking and crying for more of His revelation.

My qualification is the TRUTH. Anyone who speaks the truth is qualified to do so. And no one should be rejected when they speak the truth because they are imperfect in the things they talk about. Even with the hypocritical Pharisees, Jesus told His followers to obey what they teach but not do as they do (Matthew 23:3). The only one who is perfect is Christ, yet He calls us to go into all the world and teach others what He has taught us. That's what I am doing.

And to address the last question… I am well aware of James' admonishment concerning teachers; *"My brethren, let not many of you become teachers, knowing that we shall receive a stricter judgment"* (James 3:1, NKJV). It is a sobering thought.

Truly, teaching wasn't something I chose. It is a gift that has become a passion, particularly in the domain of Faith. I don't think I would be a very good pastor, because I lack the patience for it. But I can teach through my writings, even through my stories, which are exceptional for that. My prayer is like Paul's; that after I have preached to others, I will not find myself cast out (1 Corinthians 9:27).

Please pray for me too. As a Bible teacher, as a wife, as a mother, as a child of God; that I may fulfil the purpose for which God called me and gifted me. That, at the end of the day, despite my present trials, my own end will be a testimony of the love and power of God. Thank you, and God bless you too!

I sure hope you are encouraged to read on and pray that you will be blessed as you do. Thank you for getting your copy. Kindly drop a review for me at your preferred online retailer's site.

Love, Ufuomaee.

DISCLAIMER - The advice in this book may be ineffective for those in abusive marriages. If you have cause to believe you are in an abusive situation, you feel perpetually oppressed by your spouse, or if there is any violence ongoing, please seek professional support immediately

A for Appreciation

THERE ARE MANY WORDS beginning with A that would be great to start The Marriage ABCs with, but for me, the best is 'Appreciation.' It is an all-encompassing word because when you appreciate someone, it shows you *accept* them for who they are. You will show *affection* towards them and give them the *attention* they deserve also. Another great word is 'Agreement,' but there are other words synonymous in meaning that we can use later on.

Appreciation of your spouse is the basest and most primary duty you owe to your wife or husband. It sets the foundation for your union because, without it, there's already resentment in the marriage, as one or both will feel unwanted or not needed. So, by not appreciating your spouse, you're communicating that you would rather be single. Appreciation of your spouse cannot be overemphasised.

In case you've long been married, and you were once appreciative but have become complacent and critical towards your spouse, here are five good reasons to work on being more appreciative to your spouse:

1. You Chose Him/Her

When things get hard, we may begin to second guess our decision to marry the person we are married to. We might try to think of how he or she was not really our choice. Maybe we were pressured... Perhaps we were deceived...or we were too young to choose. But (except for cases of child marriages or arranged marriages) you did choose that person. Even if you felt it was the better of two evils at the time, you made a choice. It would be childish and irresponsible to deny your agency now.

We are always choosing from multiple options. Sometimes we are stuck between a rock and a hard place, but we make a decision based on the information available to us at any given time. And marriage calls for faithfulness...for better or for worse.

We were not deaf when the vows were read. When the pastor asked, "Does anyone know of any reason why these two cannot be joined together?", we were not in a coma, nor were we sleeping. We were most likely smiling, maybe daydreaming, possibly crying... But we were present and aware of the decision we were making. So, we need to take responsibility.

Another reason it is important to take responsibility is to respect yourself. You're not stupid. Remember why you chose him or her. Remember how you dated so many Mr Wrongs before you decided that this was the one? Remember how you told her you couldn't bear to live another day without her? Remember, remember... There were a number of factors leading to your decision, and when you remember them, you will respect the person you were when you stood at that altar to pledge unending love to your spouse. And you will be a person of integrity and fight for that love.

2. Two Are Better Than One

You may begin to think you are better off on your own. That this person is a liability; a burden or thorn in your flesh. Sometimes, you might even wonder if they are cursed...maybe they are not even Christian. Maybe they are the Devil incarnate. Maybe they are nothing so diabolical, but they do not seem to bring anything to the table, and you're sick and tired of being chained to them!

But you know, there are some people who never appreciate a good thing when it is happening to them. There are many who have forsaken their marriages, thinking they can do without their spouse, only to find that their ex is snatched up by another, who sees all the wonderful things they couldn't see, because they were blinded by their own wickedness. And unfortunately, you only begin to appreciate what you had when it's gone. You don't want to be that person.

The truth is marriage is a gift that some are unworthy of. You might be one of those who are married and unworthy of your gift because you keep complaining about it. But it is a gift. Two are better than one (Eccl 4:9-12).

You have someone who has pledged to love you for better or for worse. Someone who has committed to be your helper and your advocate. Someone who has promised to always be your friend. Isn't it nice to have a friend? A faithful friend? You are a team of two and can accomplish much more than yourself alone if you will only figure out how to work as a unit.

3. True Love is Proven in Trials

It is easy to love in good times. Piece of cake. But if you can't love in hard times, that means you are a fair-weather friend, and no friend at all. That is why the marriage covenant says, "for better or for worse." A friend is the one who rejoices with you when things are great, cries with you when things fall apart, and picks you up, encourages you, and believes in you at all times. In a trial, it is needful to have a companion, and those who come through to the other side with you are golden. You can't appreciate a friendship without trials.

What type of friend are you? In fact, what type of person are you? Even if you were shallow before Christ, when you are in Christ, you are a new creature...the old has passed away, all is now new (2 Cor 5:17). As one who lives for Christ (Gal 2:20), who imitates Christ, you cannot be a selfish person. You cannot live for yourself anymore, but you will deny yourself and consider your spouse above yourself (Phil 2:3), submitting to them in love (Eph 5:21).

Trials come as purifiers. Without them, our love is not proven, hence Jesus said that it is those who endure till the end that shall be saved (Matt 24:13). We even glory in trials because they are necessary for developing godly character, for learning patience, compassion, humility, and trust in God (Rom 5:3-5). We shouldn't run from them, nor should we invite them. But when they come, we must submit to them, and let them do their refining work in pruning our hearts, that our love may be tested and found to be true. The test is not for God; it is for you...so you may know that, without Him, you can do nothing (John 15:5).

4. You Are Not Perfect Either

It might come as a surprise, but you are not perfect. No, you're not God's gift to women/men. No, your spouse is not lucky to have you. And I might suppose, you don't deserve better either (disregard this in cases of domestic abuse). Don't think that when you leave you will find someone who will treat you better in a heartbeat. The world is filled with imperfect people like you.

We really need to get over ourselves. We feel so entitled sometimes. We might not see how much our spouse has to put up with to live with us. We might not see how unreasonable we are sometimes. I know it may feel like it, but you're not always right, and they know it...even when they apologise. They too are bearing their own cross by being faithful in the marriage (in cases where your challenges are not related to their infidelity).

You need to step out of yourself and consider it from God's perspective. Jesus gave a good analogy when He spoke about the speck and the beam (Matt 7:3-5). The speck is the difference between you and your spouse. It is so minute, it is negligible. But between you and God is an insurmountable beam. That is where God gives grace to you, that you may draw near to Him, despite your imperfection. Can't you be so gracious to your spouse?

5. God Called You to Follow His Example

God has given you a commandment, if you are a Christian, that just as He loved you, you are to love your brothers and sisters in Christ, and more so your spouse (John 13:34). **Loving your spouse should be easy, but if and when it is not, love them in obedience to Jesus. If they are a thorn in your flesh, abide with them, knowing that God's grace is sufficient for you** (2 Cor 12:7-9), and His power is made perfect in your weakness.

Just as God doesn't continually bring your faults before you, but shows you just how precious you are to Him, do likewise to your spouse. Do not constantly remember their mistakes. If you can, forget them. God separated you from your sins as far as the East is from the West (Psa 103:12), and when He looks upon you, He sees Jesus. Do so with your spouse. When you look upon them, see Jesus. Love them like they are Jesus (1 John 4:20). As you see Jesus in them, they should begin to see Jesus in themselves.

I hope these five points have convinced you that you have no justification for not appreciating your spouse. When you do so, you will begin to see them blossom and bear fruit, just like a properly loved and nourished plant would... They will change, not because you told them they were bad, or that they needed to change, but because God's love, through you, changed them. "*For it is God who works in you [and them] both to will and to do according to His good pleasure*" (Phil 2:13). They will change because they can no longer ignore the beautiful light that you are in your home (Matt 5:16).

So, if you want your marriage to work, appreciate your spouse.

To conclude, here are five simple steps you can follow to ensure that you are always fulfilling your duty to appreciate your spouse, no matter their flaws:

1. Be Grateful - This starts in your heart. Accept them for who they are. Thank God for them. Praise Him for them. Count your blessings. Think of the good things they do, and *look out* for good things they do, so you can express gratitude often.

2. Be Understanding - Try to see things from their perspective. Do not be quick to judge. Do not get angry easily. Give them the benefit of the doubt.

3. Be Humble - Do not think highly of yourself. You

could be wrong. Be willing to be taught. Consider Jesus, who, though being King, didn't come to lord it over us but served us in humility.

4. Be Encouraging - Praise them when they do good. Tell them you believe in them. Stand by them when they make mistakes, and don't rub it in their face (saying "I told you so"). Be their cheerleader and advocate, even when others are discouraging (and even when you think you have a better idea).

5. Be Loving - Be affectionate and kind to them. Kiss and touch them (even when you don't feel like it). Communicate with them as often as they are willing to engage you, and be sure to laugh and smile often. Do thoughtful things for them. Call, text, send gifts etc. Though it may feel unnatural at first, keep at it until it becomes second nature.

If you do these things, you will live to enjoy the fruit of your labour of love. If you are single and hoping to settle down, keep these in mind when choosing a mate. Is the person someone you respect enough to always appreciate them? Do you know them well enough? Do you really know yourself?

Who is your role model for love and faithfulness? Even if you don't have any role models, Jesus is your role model. He commanded us to love one another as He loved us... Can you love your spouse the way Christ loved you? Unconditionally? Forgiving all past and future wrongs?

Take some time to appreciate the love that Christ has bestowed on you and the love He has called you to. You may falter in marriage, even after considering all these things, but if you both keep your eyes on Jesus, you will certainly prevail. Love indeed conquers all!

B for Blessed to Bless

IN THE FIRST CHAPTER, we established that marriage is a gift that we ought to be grateful for. We looked at why we must not only appreciate our gift but appreciate our spouse too. I also shared five things we should be doing to show our appreciation to our spouse, which will result in a better marriage experience for both.

In this chapter, we will look more into the purpose of marriage, how it is a blessing by which we are to bless others. I'd first like to establish that both singleness and marriage are gifts (1 Cor 7:7), but they are different; like the gift of teaching and the gift of prophecy. If they are fully appreciated, if we understand why we have been so gifted, then we can use our gifts rightly in ministering to others, in obedience to God.

Marriage is a holy union (Heb 13:4); it is not a

compromise. By deciding to marry, you didn't settle for a lesser gift, but you did take on a greater responsibility (not least by the care you promised to another soul). In a similar way, the prophet has greater responsibility over every word he utters (seeing as he is speaking as by the Spirit) than the teacher, who has the opportunity to explain his choice of words. Marriage requires careful handling so that it will endure all of life's tests and bear the fruit that it was ordained to produce.

It remains that the purpose of every venture must be established at the beginning if we are to be successful in attaining our goals. Jesus also said we need to consider the costs involved, and whether we are able to go all the way, before we set sail on a mission (Luke 14:28), otherwise, we will come out as defeated fools in the end. So, we need to first appreciate the sacredness of marriage and decide if we have what it takes to make it work. We also need to understand how the vocation of marriage is already blessed and how we can use this gift to be a blessing to each other, our offspring, our community, and society in general, to the glory of God.

1. The Union is Already Blessed

When times are hard in marriage, when it seems the love is gone, it may be hard to believe that you are blessed...that your union is blessed. It is good to remember that it is. You are blessed, being a child of God. Your marriage union is both blessed and is a blessing to you and your spouse.

It is also good to remember that when God is involved in a thing, success is guaranteed. Despite the stormy waves you will encounter, you will surely make it safely across to the other side if you trust in God (the Author and Finisher of your Faith (Heb 12:2)) and do not fear (Luke

8:22-26). If you set sail apart from God, you have the strength of two humans on a divine mission. You do not have much chance of success against the inevitable storms of the sea called 'Marriage.' However, when your union is entered with the wisdom and blessing of God, you are as a "three-fold cord" that isn't easily broken (Eccl 4:12).

Even still, Christian or not, every legal marriage is recognised in Heaven, and it is God's will that it will produce the right fruits in your life and bring glory to Him. Jesus also attested to this when He acknowledged the FIVE marriages of the woman at the well while recognising that her present circumstance was not a legal marriage (John 4:17-18). We are told that if one becomes a Believer after they enter their union, God can use him or her to deliver their spouse, who doesn't yet believe (1 Cor 7:12-16). We also know that God's will is that all may be saved and come to the knowledge of the Truth (1 Tim 2:4), so even in marriages that were not ordained by God, He recognises their union, and through their marriage, He is able to teach them about His enduring love. And we know that marriage between a man and a woman is really a mystery about the Oneness of Christ and His Church (also called Bride (Eph 5:22-33)).

It is written that for a lack of vision, the people perish (Prov 29:18). **Marriages fail, not because one or both parties are cursed, or because the union is not blessed, but because the gift is mishandled.** If a wealthy father leaves an inheritance for a child who doesn't appreciate the value of what he has been given, and is not trained in how to rightly handle this endowment, it is very likely that he will not only lose his gift but the opportunity that the gift presented to be a blessing unto others. So, wisdom is profitable in all things.

2. Be A Blessing To Each Other

There is a principle we need to understand about God's blessings; they flow. They are not stagnant, poured on you to make you fat and complacent, but given that you may pay it forward, and thereby, bless others. A candle does not burn for itself but to enlighten the path of others. And by its singular flame, other candles are lit. As Jesus said, nobody lights a candle and puts it under a bushel… (Luke 11:33). Likewise, God didn't give you this gift for yourself only.

Any candle that doesn't wish to illuminate others will find that its flame will be puffed out by the slightest wind. A single candle that burns to the ground without lighting others is a disgrace and a waste. They have made no impact in their world, only consumed air and all their strength in vain. But the one that lights another, and then another until a thousand more are lit, is wise and profitable, and his legacy lives on forever through the candles that have been lit by him.

So, we are blessed that we may be a blessing to others (Gen 12:2). We are forgiven so that we may forgive. We are loved so that we may love. We are taught so that we may teach, and so on.

In marriage, the duty to bless is tied to the success of your union. You are already blessed, but you must decide to bless your spouse, knowing how greatly God has blessed you. And you should continue to bless them and strive to be a blessing (a gift) unto them, rather than a burden; never tiring of doing this good thing you have been blessed (called and ordained) to do (Gal 6:9).

Jesus said He came not to be served but to serve (Matt

20:28). We too must have a mind that we did not enter marriage to be served but to serve. The Lord also said, "*it is more blessed to give than to receive*" (Acts 20:35).

Yes, you have been blessed, and you are blessed, but when you obey the call God placed in your life with the gift He bestowed on you, by paying it forward, then you are more greatly blessed. You will be like the wise and profitable servant, who did not waste his talent (Matt 25:14-30). But if you do not rightly use your gift, then even your blessing will be taken away! So, if you do not actively bless your spouse, do not expect to enjoy or keep your marriage.

3. Children Are an Added Blessing, Not a Validation

There is a grave error in many cultures that teach that children validate marriages. Because of this, there is great pressure put on newlyweds to become fruitful in child bearing as soon as possible. If they do not conceive within an expected period of time, there is an assumption that the marriage is cursed, or that one of them (usually the wife) is cursed. And those with this mentality seek to put asunder what God has acknowledged and blessed. The damage this does to marriages, men, women, and children cannot be exaggerated.

Though children are a gift from God (Psa 127:3), they are an added blessing to a marriage that is *already* blessed. They are not the 'fruit' that determines that your marriage is good. Look, two idiots can have a baby, and they need not be married to succeed at conceiving.

Children are also not the only way that marriages can contribute to society and thereby be a blessing to the world. Child-bearing was never the primary purpose of marriage. After God made both Adam and Eve, recognising that "*it is not good for man to be alone*" (Gen

2:18), He gave *them* the command to be fruitful and replenish the Earth (Genesis 1:27-28). And we can all see that the world is REPLENISHED and even over-populated, so the expectation to bear children in marriage should be MUCH reduced for couples.

The burden to bear children has made so many miserable with the gift they already have. Husbands and wives frustrate each other because they are not content and do not realise how much they are already blessed. They cannot even use their blessing to bless each other because of this blindness. Even those with one or two children are desperate for more.

However, we know that godliness with contentment is great gain (1 Tim 6:6). Yes, even in this regard. Don't be deceived by supposed men of God who quote Scripture and tell you that God has promised to bless your marriage with children, and you shouldn't be content until He does. We are in a different dispensation with a different focus from the Israelites.

Paul's counsel is relevant here for us to get some perspective: "*But this I say, brethren, the time is short: it remaineth, that both they that have wives be as though they had none*" (1 Cor 7:29). Paul's counsel in 1 Corinthians 7 was consistently that it is better for Christians to be as he was, unmarried, because of the tribulation of the times. Our expectation of the return of Jesus, with the belief that we will soon be called Home, should cause our minds to focus on things above rather than on earthly things (1 Cor 7: 32-34, Col 3:1-3). We should not desire marriage and children as though we are of this world and seek to populate it, but we should rather desire that those who are *already* born in the flesh are *born again* in the Spirit; that ALL may be saved. I wrote more on this in my study of this chapter – https://ufuomaee.blog/a-hard-teaching.

4. Bless Your Children and Community

As a couple, a unit that is blessed by God, you ought to actively bless others; first, your children (if you have them), then your immediate family (including your family of God - the Church), and then your community (your neighbourhood, county, and country). It is said that the family is the basic unit of society, so we are to be in our smaller units what we hope to see in the larger body of society. The home is the place where we begin to exercise the gifts of God, bear the fruit of righteousness, and teach and model holiness. As we do these, we will live in the world as a light unto others.

In order to do this, the couple needs to be tightly knit, of one mind and not divided (Mark 10:8-9). When you are divided, you are not even blessing each other and cannot begin to work together to bless your children and the community. Instead, the chaos that is in you is what will be evidenced in the wider society that is made up of others like you. It is perhaps for this reason that Paul taught that leaders in the Church must be exemplary in the way they manage their homes (1 Tim 3:12).

If you want your home and your children to be blessed, then you must realise that children are not:

> **Super Glue** - you shouldn't have children with the expectation that their arrival will fix the issues in your marriage, by making you or your spouse happy. That is wicked. Your problems are not because you don't have children but because you lack love and wisdom.

> **Trophies** - children are not a prize to show off to your friends and family, as though they were an accomplishment. They are a GIFT and a great responsibility, and if you desire to have them, you need to prepare for their addition to your home so that you do

not abuse them with your ignorance or negligence.

> **Weapons** - children should not be used as weapons in an argument to hurt or control your spouse. They too are human and have their own rights.

> **Bait** - children should not be used to compel people to enter a covenant of marriage. That would be ignoring godly counsel, which requires that you count the cost before entering a marriage covenant and ascertain that you have what it takes to endure for better or worse. Even if you get pregnant outside wedlock, remember that two wrongs never made a right. A quick marriage is definitely not the solution, even if it saves you or your family some embarrassment.

> **Mediators** - children should not be burdened with mediating arguments between their parents. That is cruel.

You must bless your children by providing them with a safe, child-friendly, and homely environment. Nurture peace, love, and understanding in your home. Practice charity and forgiveness and, thereby, set an example for your children. Chastise, discipline, and train up your child in the way he or she should go (Prov 22:6). Then your children will be able to pass on the gift of your training to others they come across and will be a blessing to the world; a legacy to your name that will also bring honour to God.

5. Be a Light to the World

The duty to make your marriage work is not simply for your enjoyment of your marriage. Your faithfulness is not merely for the salvation of your spouse. Your endurance is not only for the nurturing of your children. And your labouring is not just to contribute to society's preservation. You are to abide in your marriage for all of these reasons and more.

Your marriage stands as a testament of God's love. Remember the great mystery that is marriage, being Christ and His Church. A successful marriage is a divine accomplishment because it is only a divine love that "*suffers long and is kind…does not envy…does not parade itself, is not puffed up; does not behave rudely, does not seek its own, is not provoked, thinks no evil; does not rejoice in iniquity, but rejoices in the truth; bears all things, believes all things, hopes all things, endures all things*" (1 Cor 13:4-7 NKJV). This is the love we are called to.

Your marriage is your ministry to the world that God is real and that God is love. You know that without God, you can do nothing (John 15:5). Without Him, you cannot forgive continually, you cannot be gracious and kind to those who are unloving and cruel, and you cannot be long-suffering unless you know the great reward God has for His faithful servants. So, your continuance in your marriage is an exercise of your faith in God and obedience to Him. Like I said to one sister, "this is your Christianity!" If you forsake your marriage, it is as though you have forsaken your cross. But God is gracious, and He will not let us be tempted above what we can bear (1 Cor 10:13).

When the world sees you and sees the love you share with your spouse, they should want to know about your God, and about your faith in Jesus. Because emotion is common to all, you can relate to unbelievers in this regard, showing them the great solution you have to a problem we all share - the need to be loved unconditionally. When they see your love truly conquers all, they will want it for themselves. You can preach the Gospel simply by having a marriage that reflects the love Christ has for His Church. This is the greatest fruit (or blessing) that your marriage can and should produce.

"Let your light so shine before men, that they may see your good works, and glorify your Father which is in heaven" (Matt 5:16).

C for Communicate Effectively

COMMUNICATION IS A HUGE TOPIC. I know this because it was one of the modules I did when I studied Social Work in university. Since we are relational beings, social beings, communication affects us in multi-dimensional ways, and our ability to communicate well can actually determine our success and failure in life, whether in business or in marriage. I don't think I can do the grand topic justice in one chapter, but I'll try my best in relation to marriage.

Firstly, we need to understand some basic things about communication. Communication is not speaking only. There is verbal and non-verbal communication, and it has been said that the non-verbal communication is weightier than the verbal communication. You can say a whole lot more with your silence than with words. Even though we must pay attention to our verbal communication and ensure that we utilise the right words, construct them well, and apply the right tone, pitch, and tempo to communicate ourselves well, we must also ensure that our non-verbal communication is not contradicting what we are saying with our lips.

For a simple example, you can tell someone you love them and also be rolling your eyes at the same time. Do you think they will believe you? Of course not! Your non-verbal communication, eye-rolling, conflicted with what you were saying so that what was actually *communicated* was that you do not love them, and in fact, they are quite irritating.

Another important principle about communication is that it is only complete when the message you are passing across has been received. Ideally, there should be an acknowledgement from the recipient that your message was well-received and understood. Some people think that they can shout their message, and because they shouted, it would be received and understood. An increased volume does not ensure that your actual message will be received, but it can actually confuse your message by giving the impression that you are angry. So, what happens again is that the person you're addressing doesn't take the actual content of your words into consideration as much as they take into account your yelling, so they might get mad and yell back too. That is a classic communication failure.

The study of non-verbal communication is probably as vast as the study of the English Language or any language. Within non-verbal communication, there is closed and open communication. When your spouse approaches you to talk, and you cross your hands over your chest, you are already communicating a couple of things:

1. you're not interested, so they are not welcome; and

2. you are not ready to accommodate them by changing your mind.

This is an example of closed non-verbal communication. If you want to send across a different message, then you would probably smile, lean closer, and LOOK at them.

Apart from the face to face communication, there are also things you communicate when you are not really trying to communicate. **You have to be aware that you are ALWAYS communicating something, whether you are happy, angry, worried, or irritated. Knowingly or unknowingly, you are sending messages to your spouse about what is going on with you and how you feel about them.** Knowing this is important because you can now take control of the messages you are communicating and also take responsibility when you pass across the wrong message carelessly.

Let me present another example. You come home from work and carelessly slam the door. Your wife in the kitchen receives the message that you've had a bad day. She too has had a stressful day and came back early to cook. You shout from the living room, "I'm hungry! Any food?" She receives the message that you're impatient and unappreciative of what she does for you. You switch on the TV, open your laptop, and get locked in your own world and don't bother to look at her face when she finally brings your dinner. How do you think your wife will translate all that you have been communicating carelessly? Do you suppose you might have an argument that night?

So, communication requires that we empathize with others, put ourselves in their shoes, and consider how they might receive a message we are trying to communicate. That will result in us being more sensitive, thoughtful, diplomatic, and affirming when we interact with them. Before we spout off about how horrible our day has been, we might want to own our feelings so that we do not offload on our unsuspecting spouse. You should rather begin with an affectionate, "Honey, how was your day?" even if you just had the day from hell. Then after you have LISTENED and RESPONDED to them, not simply waiting for them to finish their long story while thinking about how you will tell them what an awful day you had, you can then begin to give an account of your day...once again, owning your feelings.

A major barrier to effective communication is that we do not listen. If we do not listen, we will not receive the message that is communicated. Again, listening isn't simply about verbal communication. You need to be attentive to other messages that they are not communicating verbally. If someone is visibly in pain, and they say they are fine, you know that something is wrong. If someone keeps repeating a phrase or they seem to be saying the same thing in different ways, perhaps they are trying to communicate that you do not understand them, and you need to stop and listen.

In an argument, it is very easy not to listen. Mostly because you think you are right, and because you think that they are not listening. They may be listening and still disagree with you, and you have to make sure that YOU are listening and not thinking of your comeback. If you are both listening, then you should be able to come to a conclusion on the matter, even if it is to agree to disagree on that issue. The main thing is that you and your partner were able to express your own viewpoints in a respectful, loving, and supportive atmosphere that resulted in both of you better understanding and appreciating where the other was coming from.

Finally, another major area of communication in marriage is the concept of Love Languages, which was made popular by Gary Chapman's book, **"The Five Love Languages - How to Express Heartfelt Commitment to Your Mate"** (REF 1). Many of you will be aware of this, and you can read up on it via the Internet or by getting the book. It has been quite ground breaking in its impact in helping couples to have better communication and show love and appreciation to each other. The five love languages are:

1. Word of Affirmation - We all like to be appreciated, but if this is your dominant love language, you are big on encouragement. You want to be told you're a good mother or wife, or good father or husband. You want to be acknowledged for what you do, so you need to hear "Thanks for doing..." Hearing the words stops you from guessing and wondering if they noticed or even cared, and it's okay to need the affirmation.

2. Acts of Service - We all like to be taken care of, but if this is your dominant love language, you are big on pampering. You want to be treated like a king or a queen. You like your spouse to be helpful around the house, do nice things for you without you having to ask, and actually *enjoy* this service too. For you, actions speak louder than words.

3. Receiving Gifts - We all like to receive nice things, but if this is your dominant love language, you are big on thoughtful gifts. You want to know that your spouse is thinking of you often, and the fact that they went to the trouble to purchase something they thought or knew you would like tells you that you are loved. It isn't because you can't get it yourself, but that it cost them not only money but time and care to pick out your special gift.

4. Quality Time - We all like to spend time with the one we love, but if this is your dominant love language, you are big on attention. Nothing says "I love you" more than your spouse choosing to spend the day with you, doing the things you love to do, and actually enjoying it like you do. It's not just about the opportunity to talk but also the shared moments of silence, relaxation, or pleasure. It makes you feel connected, in sync.

5. Physical Touch - We all like to be touched and kissed, but if this is your dominate love language, you are big on affectionate touches. You like public displays of affection, holding hands as you walk along the street, kissing as often as you think about it, and making love a lot. Being able to express your desire for your spouse through intimate touches and caresses is important to you, and when they touch you, you also feel desirable.

Each person is unique, and you need to understand your spouse to know what love language they appreciate best, so you can communicate love and affection to them in a way they won't miss. If your spouse loves to spend quality time talking, and you think that buying them expensive things communicates your love and appreciation better, you are still going to have a disgruntled and unsatisfied spouse. And you might end up thinking that they are ungrateful when, instead of "I love you," they heard, "I'm too busy, manage this."

While both spouses need to make every effort to learn their spouse's love language and communicate it to them regularly, my personal feeling is that where there is a lack, the man needs to lead the way. Women reciprocate love. So, if you desire to be touched and made love to, in order to know that you are loved by your woman, you need to first reach out to her by speaking her language. If she likes to go out and eat, take her out. If she likes to receive thoughtful gifts, be sure to come home with flowers, chocolates, or something nice every now and then. If she prefers a handyman, and she finds you sexiest when you're fixing things, then be on the look-out for opportunities to be helpful around the house. Yes, even doing the dishes and offering to cook.

You will probably not find that you and your wife have the same dominant love language, because I believe we all like every one of the five expressions, some more than others. However, if you and your wife are exactly the same, great! But don't take this for granted. People change. Even if you don't change, she might change. Especially after having children. She may not want to go out as much. She may prefer you to be more hands on. She may prefer you to be more affirmative, reassuring, and appreciative of what she does.

Ladies, men change too. Constantly review and adjust, to ensure that you are always communicating love and appreciation in the most effective way to your spouse.

So, to round this up, I would like to talk briefly about what we should expect to achieve with effective communication in marriage. Like all things, communication can be abused. We can have unrealistic expectations and make ourselves miserable trying to use a spoon to do a job that requires a shovel. Communication is a tool, and when well used, it saves marriages. But there are other things at play, mainly our submission and relationship with God.

1. Communicate for Unity, not Absolute Agreement - Effective and good communication between spouses will enable better bonding between them and ensure that they are united. Being united doesn't mean that you will agree on every single issue. You are not clones. Your unity comes from having the same vision for your marriage and being submissive to each other. With that established, you will be able to drop certain arguments to keep the peace.

2. Communicate for Understanding, not Absolute Knowledge - You should communicate with the aim of learning more about your spouse and coming to understand them; how they think, what makes them happy or sad, etc. It isn't so that you can write a manual on them. Let there be some mystery. Trust your spouse to be their own person, knowing that they are already submitted to God. Only God knows and should know everything about us, and we shouldn't approach communication as if we are preparing for an exam on our marriage.

3. Communicate for Care and Concern, not Control - You should communicate to show that you care about your spouse and are concerned for what is happening in their lives. You should be their number one confidant, and they shouldn't be shy nor afraid to open up to you, because they feel you are going to take over and be controlling. For example, if your spouse is telling you about a problem at work, listen attentively, and if you have any ideas share them, but don't push them and tell them they should do it your way. That's controlling.

4. Communicate for Intimacy, not Insecurity - Sometimes, when we communicate, we reveal our insecurities. This may be a sign of lack of trust or emotional instability. We should communicate to grow in intimacy with our spouse, not to heap them with burdens we should rather lay at God's feet. They can be your prayer partner, they can counsel you, but don't think they can handle your anxieties. They've got theirs too. The Bible says, "*Cast all your anxiety on [God], because He cares for you*" (1 Peter 5:7).

5. Communicate for Restoration, not to Accuse and Convict - Offenses will come. Grievances will arise. But in all things, remain gracious and kind. Remain humble and wise. Do not use communication as a tool to convict your spouse, with interrogations as though you are in court. The Devil is our accuser, so try to come with the recognition that you could be wrong, and seek to understand and to restore your relationship in love.

In closing, communication is an essential tool for building up your relationship with your spouse. We are told that "*the wise woman builds her house, but the foolish tears it down with her own hands*" (Proverbs 14:1). While men are commanded to love their wives as Christ loves the Church, women are obligated to trust their husbands (Eph 5:22-33). We need to be supportive of their role as leaders in our marriage and home and give them room to lead.

While we are both to submit to one another, as we submit to God (Eph 5:21), the woman is also burdened with the duty of showing submissive respect to her husband. She must respect his authority as the leader in the home while he is submitted to Christ. Therefore, as one who is submitted to Christ, the husband must be humble and serve his wife because the Son of Man came not to be served but to serve (Matt 20:28), and he who wishes to be great must become the least (Matt 20:26).

It remains that both, husband and wife, owe each other due courtesy and respect when communicating with each other. Love is not rude, nor is it self-seeking (1 Cor 13:5). We must always, in every circumstance, perform our duty of love to one another, and thereby fulfil God's law (Rom 13:8). And if we do, our home shall be a haven and a place where the peace that surpasses all understanding abides. May the grace of God be with you and bless your marriage.

D for Die Daily to Self

THIS IS PROBABLY THE HARDEST thing for anybody to do, but it is also the most rewarding act of love. Jesus taught us this principle of losing to gain, through His death on the Cross, where He gave up His life to gain the world (John 3:16). He gave an illustration of this spiritual principle, which is applicable to us as His followers and profitable also in marriage. He said:

"Truly, truly, I tell you, unless a kernel of wheat falls to the ground and dies, it remains only a seed; but if dies, it bears much fruit" (John 12:24).

This is the principle of the Cross, the Wisdom of God, and it has great power. Many know it as the sowing principle... You reap what you sow. You get what you put in... No pain, no gain, and so on.

Jesus taught His disciples to follow His example by bearing their own crosses, saying, "*If anyone would come after Me, he must deny himself and take up his cross and follow Me. For whoever wants to save his life will lose it, but whoever loses his life for My sake will find it...*" (Matt 16:24-25). Without denying ourselves, we cannot be His disciples, and we cannot bear His fruit.

We, who make up the Body of Christ, are called the Bride of Christ. Jesus showed us the love of a Husband, by laying down His life for us to redeem us and to bless us. Paul tells all Christian husbands that they ought to imitate Christ in this regard and lay down their lives for their wives...loving them as their own body, even as Christ loves the Church (Eph 5:25-26). This requires great humility and brokenness. To be obedient in this regard, a husband must die daily to self, putting to death the deeds of his flesh and submitting to the Spirit of Christ. They should have this mind:

"I have been crucified with Christ; and it is no longer I who live, but Christ lives in me; and the life which I now live in the flesh I live by faith in the Son of God, who loved me and gave Himself up for me" (Gal 2:20).

Wives are not left out. While Christ led the way, by dying to redeem His Bride, He also commanded us to forfeit our own lives to gain eternal life. While we were yet unworthy sinners, Christ died for us (Rom 5:8), and we show our love for Him through obedience, submission, and by forsaking all to Him in return. In like manner, a wife responds to the love her husband shows her through daily dying to himself...by following suit. She is called to show submission and honour to her husband, who represents Christ, as the head of their home (Eph 5:22-24), and she shows her devotion and trust in God by the love and respect she shows her husband.

"If anyone says, 'I love God,' but hates his brother, he is a liar. For anyone who does not love his brother, whom he has seen, cannot love God, whom he has not seen" (1 John 4:20).

The Bible presents us with this challenge because many claim to be spiritual but are not. It is by obedience that our love for righteousness is proven. If we cannot die daily in loving submission to our spouse, how can we claim to die daily to Christ? We cannot.

So, what does it mean to die to self daily? What does it look like, and what is it not? I want to explore that with you now.

DYING DAILY IS:

1. Smashing your pride. Pride and love have no business and no positive relationship. If you seek to love, you must forego your pride. You must humble yourself. This will mean that if and when you do wrong, you are quick to admit it to yourself, confess it to your spouse, repent of it to God, and if possible, repair the damage caused by sin promptly. You will not be ashamed to own up to your fault if ever it is pointed out to you, nor would you have to be compelled to apologise. You will also be quick to forgive, remembering how much you have been forgiven. You won't seek your own but only seek what will bring glory to God and joy to your spouse.

2. Doubting yourself. This is similar to the first point, but it is more specifically about opinions and perspectives and how we deal with our differences in marriage. Everyone thinks they are right. Everyone. And if no one ever doubted themselves, there would be no understanding, no resolution, no agreement, and no reconciliation. You will be like two parallel lines that never meet, or worse, are divergent, drifting further and further apart. It is therefore important for everyone to doubt themselves. You could be wrong. Try to understand where your spouse is coming from in a disagreement. Try to see things from their perspectives.

Wear their shoes for a while, and be compassionate, knowing that you also need them to do the same for you.

3. Dropping the argument. Sometimes, even when you have smashed your pride and doubted yourself, there seems no resolution to the problem you are facing. It may be that the other person is not rigorously dying to self, but it isn't your place to crucify them. Dying to self is a choice, an act of love that each person must willingly do. If you're getting nowhere, consider dropping the issue - if it isn't of great moral significance. Forsake your opinion. You can agree to disagree, or you can decide to submit to their way and trust God to lead you both.

In most cases, the wives, who are followers of their husbands, will need to do this first. But men who are sensitive to their wife's needs will understand the areas where they are more knowledgeable or resilient. They will submit to their counsel for the sake of keeping peace and maintaining positive feeling in the home. Sometimes dropping the argument is a form of leadership, which says, "our unity is more important than me being right all the time."

4. Changing your mind. There's a saying that "*if you can't change your mind, why have one?*" (REF 4a). Proverbs also says, "*A fool hath no delight in understanding, but that his heart may discover itself*" (chap 18; vs 2). People who are really thinking...who are really listening...who are growing in understanding will change their minds. Unless you think you know it all... Unless you think that you are the most mature you will ever be? So, you have to be ready and willing to change your mind when having a disagreement or misunderstanding with your spouse. With the right attitude, you will listen to learn, and you will respond to what you have learnt by adapting your behaviour accordingly. Your spouse will also appreciate it when they observe the changes in you, because it not only shows that you are listening but that you understand them, appreciate them, respect them, and love them.

5. Forgiving all offences. How many times a day should you forgive someone who offends you? You know the answer, and it isn't 70 x 7. Jesus was just trying to communicate that as often as someone offends you and comes to you for forgiveness, you ought to pardon them. Why? Because that's what God does for you. Can you count how many times you have offended God? Even knowingly? Even repeating the same offence over and over? Jesus said that if we will not forgive, we will not be forgiven (Matt 6:15).

So, marriage, especially, calls for graciousness. We ought to be ready to forgive, just as God is ready to forgive us...even future sins. Before they even think to say "I'm sorry." Saying "I'm sorry" is for THEIR benefit, not yours. So that their conscience will be clear before God, and they can enjoy a restored relationship with you. But even before they say sorry, forgive. Because that's what God does. And forgiveness is good for your soul (Heb 12:15). In time, you will hardly be offended because you are so GOOD at forgiving and *forgetting*.

6. Serving in love. Give, give, and give some more. Enjoy the labour of a servant because Jesus said the greatest among you shall be the servant (Luke 22:26). Do not labour as unto men, but as unto God (Col 3:23-25). Even when you don't feel like it. **Even when they don't 'deserve' it. Even when you are hardly appreciated for it. Keep serving and doing good to your spouse.** Let it become second nature. You will see that you will build them up...and as you build them up, you are building yourself up too - because YOU ARE ONE. There's no benefit they will enjoy at the top that you will not share. So, be faithful with the little things, and do not despair in well-doing (Gal 6:9).

7. Going the extra mile. This is an extension of number six. Jesus taught us that if we are compelled to go one mile when we would rather not, we should go ahead and go two miles (Matt 5:41). Don't just do what is demanded of you, or what is expected of you. Go the extra mile. Put your all into it.

When you prepare that meal, let it taste like you prepared it for the King Himself and not your ungrateful husband. Don't worry about burning out because, if you have the mind that you are doing it to the glory of God, God will bless you with strength to keep glorifying His name in that way. Draw your strength from Christ, by Whom you can do all things (Phil 4:13).

8. Giving your spouse credit. This is another way you can smash your pride. Often when we accomplish something, especially when we carried the bulk of the weight, if not all...we find it hard to acknowledge or celebrate those in a supportive role in our lives. We have to actively resist this temptation and consider what influence, what benefit their presence gave to our ability to achieve our feat, even if it was their negativity that spurred us on... There must be some credit that can be attributed to our spouse.

And I think, if we think about it, it won't simply be negative. Maybe they gave you the freedom to pursue your passion. Perhaps they inspired the idea, supported you with their approval, or helped with brainstorming the idea. Maybe they attended to other demanding things so you could focus on your dream. Whatever it is, share credit, as you would with God, knowing that without Him, you could do nothing. Don't hog the glory.

9. Choosing to trust. It can be tempting to give in to doubt. It can be tempting to second guess your spouse and wonder if they are lying to you. If they are cheating on you. If they are enjoying someone else's company more...or hiding out at work. Because you are not with your spouse all the time, if there are problems in your marriage, trust is one of the first things to go. But once trust goes, there's hardly anything else to build upon.

Even if you think it makes you look foolish, and you would hate to be the last to know that your spouse has been unfaithful, resist the temptation to snoop. Trust, and treat them as though you trust them. Let your home be an inviting place they would want to return to, not one where they feel constantly interrogated or nagged. There is such a thing as a self-fulfilling prophecy, so don't tear down your marriage with your suspicions. The greatest thing at stake isn't your pride, it is your marriage.

10. Doing the right thing. The spirit and the flesh are constantly at odds (Gal 5:17). The flesh will pull you one way, maybe to feed your pride and flirt with your secretary, but the spirit knows that it is better to flee temptation and consider those you might hurt with your wrong deeds. Though we are tempted to do wrong, we must constantly resist our flesh and do the right thing. Our flesh may tell us we are being unreasonable, unrealistic, overly cautious, overly religious... But you must know that your enemy is a roaring lion seeking whom to devour (1 Pet 5:8). He will say just about anything to get his way and get you to let down your guard and do what is wrong. Rather, tune in to God's wisdom, and remember that love doesn't delight in evil (1 Cor 13:6). Also, if your spouse is trying to get you to do what is wrong, this is a time to stand for Christ (Luke 14:26) and do what is right, remembering that we are called to forsake them as well as ourselves in order to follow Jesus.

DYING DAILY IS NOT:

1. Self-hatred. You are a child of God, worthy of love and respect. Before you can expect others to love and respect you, you need to treat yourself with love and respect. Self-denial doesn't mean treating yourself as less than others, but overcoming our tendency towards selfishness and *choosing* to put the needs of others before our own, just like a servant (Phil 2:3-8).

2. False humility. This is an extension of number one. False humility, while trying to counter pride, actually destroys confidence. You can be confident without being proud. You can acknowledge your strengths, as well as your weaknesses, and use this knowledge to better serve others. Don't talk yourself out of a promotion or blessing by trying to sound 'humble'! Also don't devalue the contributions you make to your home.

3. Pretending to change. If you really haven't changed your mind, self-denial doesn't call for faking it. That is deceptive, and it destroys trust. It is also mocking, as your spouse will think you do not actually respect them enough to tell them the truth. It is better to agree to disagree, and find another point of agreement, than to say you will change and make a mockery of your relationship.

4. Suppressing your feelings. Your feelings matter. You are in the relationship too. And you're not the house rug. Express yourself and your feelings with respect. Be prayerful and humble about addressing offenses. Burying your feelings won't make them go away. They will only fester, grow, and manifest themselves in a blow-out another day. Use effective communication to ensure that your needs are also being attended to in your marriage.

5. Point-scoring. Yes, by all means, try to out-serve your spouse. Try to be the one who backs down first in an argument and who forgives easiest. But don't keep score! It's really not a competition. You also want your spouse to do better, to grow closer to God, and to enjoy the rewards of wisdom and humility. You are a team, both working to have the best marriage, so don't see your spouse as your competitor.

It is a very simple principle. If you want to be alone or lonely in marriage then, by all means, keep your pride. Don't compromise for anybody. Don't invest in your relationship. You will eventually die...lonely and miserable. But if you want a happy marriage, filled with love and every good thing, let yourself be spilled generously on the altar of your marriage. Hold nothing good back. Forgive without keeping a record of wrongs. Give love unconditionally. And you will reap a great harvest of love in your marriage.

E for Expectations, Expectations

UNREALISTIC EXPECTATIONS in marriage have been called the 'Silent Marriage Killer.' This dishonourable title is actually well earned because our expectations pave the way for disappointment, bitterness, and resentment, which steal our joy from savouring whatever is good in our marriage. So, it is important that as we guard our hearts with all diligence, we must also guard our expectations in marriage (Prov 4:23).

Some people say that if you have no expectations, you will not be disappointed, but I would disagree. Having some *reasonable* expectations is good and needed. There are some basic things one should expect in marriage and some things one should reject. Expectations are a type of hope, and without hope, there is no sustenance of life and joy. You are as the living dead. And you can also destroy the hope and joy of your spouse if you act like you care about nothing and nothing moves you. They will stop making efforts to please you or to change or even to appreciate you in the marriage. And your low or zero expectations for a blissfully unhappy marriage will *still* be dashed!

Yes, it is safe to assume that it could get worse. You can expect to be disappointed, whatever the expectations you have for your marriage. So, if your expectations are pitifully low, expect worse. But if your expectations are better than average, you might get average and still be content. However, if your expectations are the thing of fairy tales, then expect even less than average because nothing demotivates someone more than trying to live up to an unattainable standard. They will give up the farce, and you will be sorely disappointed.

So, have expectations, but let them to realistic, reasonable, moderate, and attainable. But most importantly, lay them at the right place...at the feet of Jesus, not at your spouse's feet. The truth is Jesus is the only one we can trust with our expectations. We are to lay all our hope in Him and cast all our burdens at His feet (Psa 55:22). With men, you can bet on being disappointed, but with God, you can bet on being *pleasantly* surprised. Humans let you down, but God shows you a better way.

The other thing to remember is to expect the unexpected. Life is not predictable. The only constant is change, and in change, we have security. Your spouse may disappoint you, and they may yet surprise you. Expect the unexpected. Life may favour you, or you may be knocked down constantly. Expect the unexpected. Marriage is for better or for worse, richer or poorer. Though you may start off one way, you may enter into the bitter end and struggle to get out. But you must get out together because you are in it together. Expect your faith and love to be tested in every way.

But whatever life throws at you, whatever your spouse does to you, whatever temptations you face along the way, remember that you have an Anchor (Heb 6:19), who will establish you and ground you so that you will not be utterly destroyed and can rise again. If you are rooted in Him, if you abide in Him, despite the storms of life, you will still have joy and hope, and you will *grow* in love, because He is Love, and bear much fruit (John 15:1-5).

You can expect Him to deliver you out of all your troubles... (Psa 34:17) You can expect Him to stay with you and comfort you in your loneliest and darkest moments... (Isa 41:10) You can expect Him to bring to completion the good work He has begun in you (Phil 1:6).

Let us now look at five reasonable expectations we can have for our marriage, and then look at some unreasonable expectations we may carry into marriage.

Five Reasonable Expectations:

1. Companionship. The first reason for marriage is companionship. God saw that it was not good for man to be alone, so He made him a companion in woman (Gen 2:18). It is therefore reasonable to expect companionship from your marriage. Your spouse should be your first *and* best friend, but least of all...they should be a friend. They should be someone you can trust, someone you love, and someone you like. And you should be the same to them. You will spend your marriage building on this basic foundation of friendship, and God's work in your marriage is to make you MORE than friends, but ONE entity. He does the binding, while you do the cleaving (Gen 2:24).

2. Respect. This is the basic unit of love. You can't love someone you do not first respect. In fact, if you disrespect them, you act as one who *hates* the person, by belittling them, thinking little of them, hindering them, and altogether opposing their rights to joy, love, and peace. Every human being deserves to be respected and have their rights protected and upheld. Love doesn't thrive in putting down others or overpowering the weak but in showing compassion and hope for them to overcome every hindrance to their success. In marriage, you need to show greater honour (or respect) to your spouse than you would any other human being. If you fail to respect your spouse, you are disrespecting (and hating) yourself (Eph 5:28-29) and sabotaging your marriage. Give and expect respect in your marriage.

3. Tribulation. Trials will come (1 Pet 4:12-13). It is a promise of life in a fallen world. You will be tempted. The Bible says that there is no temptation that is uncommon to man (1 Cor 10:13). There is really nothing new under the Sun (Eccl 1:9). Apart from natural trials and normal temptations, you will also face evil persecution because of your faith and the state of the world (John 15:20; Matt 10:22). You will come across those who seek to destroy your marriage, through the spreading of lies, laying down of traps, and other forms of attack. It can be spiritually motivated, and it can also simply be a natural coincidence. But expect tribulation. Expect to be tried and tested. But "*consider it pure joy, brothers and sisters, whenever you face trials of many kinds, because you know that the testing of your faith produces perseverance. Let perseverance finish its work so that you may be mature and complete, not lacking anything*" (Jam 1:2-4).

4. Maturity. God uses trials to build up our spiritual man (1 Pet 1:6-7). Through trials, we learn to trust in God, to be dependent on Him, to submit to His wisdom, to imitate Him in love, knowing that love conquers all (1

Cor 13:8). We progress from a place of entitlement to a place of servitude, just as Christ left the glorious riches of Heaven to serve the lowliest in the world (Phil 2:6-8). Even as we bear fruit by abiding in Jesus, we must be pruned so that we can bear more. So, we keep learning and growing into the image of Christ.

Marriage, with all its challenges, is the greatest place to learn what love means. Expect to grow up in marriage. Many enter thinking they know what love is or means. They don't have a clue. **It is in the serving, being broken, forgiving, depending, submitting, building up, trusting, and long-suffering that we learn what love is and what it demands; that we are able to mature in love and bear fruit.** Appreciate and submit to the process of growth.

5. Victory. Expect to be victorious in marriage. Yes, you can! Don't look at the statistics, because the statistics tell of those who didn't believe, not of those who, through faith, made it to the promised land. This is a reasonable expectation because, as we already established, YOU ARE BLESSED. And your marriage is blessed. And the Lord is looking to use your marriage to grow your character, strengthen your faith, build up your spouse, train up your children, and teach the world about His enduring love. He is with you, and He wants you to succeed. All you have to do is trust and obey and abide in Him. For without Him, you can do nothing (John 15:5). Victory is not dependent on the amount of trials, nor the nature of these trials, but on the might and glory of your God. His word cannot return to Him void (Isa 55:11). Believe in it, and fight for your marriage.

Five Unreasonable Expectations:

1. Soul Mate. I will not tell you it is impossible, but it is

HIGHLY unlikely that you have a soul mate, and that you will meet your soul mate in your lifetime, or that you will even marry such a person. You will probably lose out on finding a GOOD partner, because they didn't meet up to this great expectation for a match made in heaven. It is better to look for someone who is mature, who shares the same faith and vision for life and marriage as you, and someone who is attractive to you, who you love to be around, than to look for your perfect match. And even if you think you found your perfect match in your spouse, please expect to be disappointed because, as long as they are still human, they have flaws, and you will soon find them. It is better not to hold anyone to such unrealistic standards.

2. Worship. It is one thing to expect honour in marriage. It is quite another to expect worship. This is an abuse of love and respect. Only God is worthy of worship and is entitled to demand worship. You are not God, and neither is your spouse. Do not place them on a pedestal to worship nor let yourself be placed on a pedestal to be worshiped. It is normal to want to be adored, admired, and respected, but we have to be careful because, in this fallen world, even our normal desires are easily corrupted with pride. It has been said that *"with great power comes great responsibility"* (REF 4b), and none of us is able to handle the responsibility that is laid on us when we are exalted in worship. We must learn to think humbly of ourselves and be content with receiving pure love and respect. If you will not humble yourself, expect to be humbled (Matt 23:12).

3. Ease and Luxury. No matter how much we are warned that marriage is not easy, that we will be tried...there is no shortage of those who get the wake-up call after saying "I do!" Within a matter of weeks, they are 'shocked' by the reality and simplicity of marriage, compared to their glamourous imaginations. This is especially hard because, in romance and courtship, you may have been promised provision, protection, security, and stability by a well-meaning fellow or by someone who was enjoying such a lifestyle before they married you. But SHIT HAPPENS. If you do not expect the unexpected, you won't be able to survive when an outcome you never expected or planned for happens. Your pampered personality will take a beating. Your spouse will be shocked by your naivety and your fickleness when you start complaining, accusing, and reacting badly to a situation you may have dealt with better if you had been more realistic in your expectations. So, expect to be shocked by life.

4. No Change. If there is one constant in life, it is change. Yet many people enter marriage thinking that they will never change, their spouse will never change, their circumstances will never change (at least only get better), and their feelings will never change. But life changes us daily. As we learn, we change. As we watch, we change. As we read, we change. We are constantly having to change our perspectives, ideologies, and expectations.

Consider the changes technology has made on our relationships, not simply our businesses. Change is not always visible, but like the Earth that spins on its axis, it is happening without our knowledge nor assistance. You will change. Your spouse will change. Your circumstances will change. Your feelings will change. But God's wisdom will not. It is His wisdom that will sustain you through all your changes and make them have POSITIVE rather than negative effects on your life and on the world (Rom 8:28). Expect change.

5. Failure. Only a fool starts a mission expecting failure (Luke 14:28-30). Yet, that is the attitude we are teaching people with the idea that divorce is okay, and in fact, they should plan ahead for divorce so that it is more favourable to them when it happens. Like I already said, if you have such low expectations, expect to have a crash landing sooner than expected. Those who enter marriage must be of the mind that it will and *must* work. They must envision every exit barred in a place where every tool for their success is buried for them to discover and utilise. Once they realise that there is no way out, they will learn by compulsion how to live in peace with one another. Once they begin to discover these hidden tools, they will begin to enjoy the *adventure* that is their marriage and will soon forget about the barred exits. In fact, they won't want to leave at all, even if the exit was to be opened, because they have allowed themselves time to mature in love and their attitudes towards each other have changed for the better. Like the song by Jimmy Cliff says, "*You can get it if you REALLY want... But you must try, try and try, try and try... You'll succeed at last!*" (REF 5a).

It is important to curb and fine-tune our expectations, even at the point of dating and courtship. Unfortunately, this is a period when people who don't really know who they are or what they are capable of market themselves to their potential spouse. They present a very good image, they go over and beyond themselves to win the other's affections, they are in their best behaviour, intentionally or unintentionally deceiving and being deceived about what awaits them in marriage. So, by the time you enter marriage, the acts cease, the scales fall off, and you are faced with reality...a reality you were not expecting and were not prepared for. This can be heart-breaking, and if not rightly handled, the two people who just pledged eternal love to each other may be eagerly trying to get their marriage annulled.

It is therefore important to discuss your expectations for marriage *before* you enter marriage. You need to be brutally honest with yourself and your partner. This is the place for addressing what you *just can't stand* and what *you can't live without*, and the time where you will need to consider if your expectations are reasonable or not, and change them before marriage forces you to change or drop them out of resentment.

You need to also consider that your knowledge of yourself is not whole, and expect that, not only will you surprise your spouse with who you really are, you will also shock yourself about what you are capable of when trials and temptations come. Remember, "*let him who thinks he stands, take heed lest he falls*" (1 Cor 10:12). Marriage counselling is very important for helping couples to honestly thrash out these issues and assess their compatibility and chances of success in marriage.

Marriage is like an unexplored country. You have to be ready to learn, adjust, and keep learning from day one. Before marriage, you were presented with a brochure about all the good things that await you in this country. You saw the rivers, the beaches, the city life, the business prospects, the resorts, and theme parks. You got really excited and couldn't wait. You overlooked the fine print, which says that the land has several undiscovered landmines... You overlooked the fine print that says that there is a dormant volcano that may erupt during your stay there... You overlooked the fine print about some unresolved political conflicts in the land. Really, I can't say this enough...expect the unexpected!

On a final note, expect to enjoy getting to know who you are as a person, a spouse, and a parent. Expect to enjoy the journey of marriage, however turbulent. It will not be boring! Expect to be challenged emotionally, intellectually, and even sexually. If you have been obedient to God to abstain from sex before marriage, you will soon discover that sex is not all you imagined it would be. It really isn't as exotic as it appears in the movies. You will need to work at it, humbly and selflessly, so that you and your spouse are both fulfilled sexually in your marriage.

Don't let your unrealistic expectations make you unhappy in a *good* marriage. Appreciate your marriage for what it is and your spouse for who they are. Lay your expectations before God, and focus on serving and blessing your spouse rather than being served or worrying about being happy. No one can make you happy or unhappy. Happiness is a choice; it is a matter of perspective.

F for Friends Forever

WHEN YOU THINK ABOUT your favourite things in life, having friends must be right up there with eating cake. Friends satisfy our most basic needs for acceptance, belonging, and care. Friends tell us that we are worthwhile...we are appreciated and we are loved. Everybody needs a friend. And there is no friend like the one who sticks by you through thick and thin.

Marriage is a beautiful arrangement where someone pledges their friendship to you, not for a day, not for a while, but FOREVER, through every circumstance. Until death separates you, you will be the best of friends. And even beyond the grave, though your marriage doesn't continue, your friendship would continue in the heavenly realm. **So, your friendship does not simply ensure that you have a companion in this life, but it also guarantees you have a**

partner to help you to be faithful and not to falter in your faith walk through life.

Friends have each other's backs. They look out for one another. They keep you standing when the world tries to knock you down. They stand by you and care for you when everyone else walks away. They fight for you and stand beside you when trouble comes knocking. They celebrate with you when you succeed, and they encourage and motivate you when you don't so that you won't give up, but you will keep trying until you are victorious.

It is written that:

"Two are better than one; because they have a good reward for their labour. For if they fall, the one will lift up his fellow: but woe to him that is alone when he falleth; for he hath not another to help him up. Again, if two lie together, then they have heat: but how can one be warm alone? And if one prevails against him, two shall withstand him; and a threefold cord is not quickly broken" (Eccl 4:9-12).

There is so much that could be said for friendship, but in this chapter, our focus is on friendship in marriage. "*Can two walk together unless they agree?*" (Amos 3:3). The answer is, of course, "no." One of the most basic things about friends is their agreement - common ground. Friends who promise to be friends forever must share a united vision for their future, not just agreement in the present. They should have much more agreement than disagreement if they want to spend their years enjoying and building on their friendship, rather than fighting and defending their union.

There are FIVE Fun Facts about friendship in marriage that I would love to share with you. Funny thing is how they all start with the letter "F". It will help us to remember them.

FOREVER FRIENDS - Marriage calls for better or for worse, until death do you part. You're in this for the long haul, so pick your friend wisely. Remember, your family was chosen for you by God, but *you* choose your friends.

Don't blame God later. Want to spot the one you should spend the rest of your life with? Look out for the friend who sticks closer than a brother (Prov 18:24).

FORGIVING FRIENDS - No two people can walk together forever without regularly forgiving one another. Because nobody is perfect, not even you. Times will come when you need forgiveness from your spouse, or you need to forgive your spouse. Look out for the gracious ones, and make sure you are counted in their number too, if you want to live happily ever after. Remember that forgiveness is a gift you give yourself...not simply a duty of love.

FAITHFUL FRIENDS - The marriage relationship is unique. The Bible says that our bodies no longer belong to just us but to our spouses (1 Cor 7:4). And if your body belongs to your spouse, it would be a great wickedness to give it to another to abuse. Friends who wish to stay together forever ought to honour their marriage bed (Heb 13:4) and keep themselves only for their spouse. They also guard their hearts from others, knowing that once the heart is conquered, the body is not far behind.

FAMILY FRIENDS - Once you are married, you have moved from mere friends to family. Family ties are strong and protected by law in ways ordinary friendships cannot expect to be. They say, "*blood is thicker than water*" (REF 4c), and they are right. Watching over your family is like watching over your own body, most especially the unique relationship between a man and his wife (Eph 5:22-33), who have become ONE flesh (Matt 19:5-6). And even though you can have a best friend who is closer than a family member, a best friend who *is* a family member is the best of all, not least because they have more authority, liberty, and *reason* to act in defence of you always.

FORTUNE FRIENDS - So, I made this one up. But I think it will round off our five fun facts well. It is connected to the family friends because, in marriage, the saying goes, "*whatever is mine is yours.*" How wonderful is that?! Whether little or much, you share your wealth together equally. Your progress is his progress. Her success is your success. And if ever one of you is down, you have just as much reason to labour to get out of the trench together. Because your fortunes are tied forever, you are less likely to leave the other in the lurch and more likely to overcome and succeed in all that you do together. This is also important when you think of eternal life, a shared fortune that you can and should help each other attain to.

So, this chapter is short, sweet, and simple. We all know what we want in a friend, and that is EXACTLY what we should put into our marriage relationship. The law of love is summed up in this, "*...whatever you wish that others would do to you, do also to them*" (Matt 7:12). Do you wish to be forgiven? Then forgive. Do you wish to be understood? Then seek to understand. Do you wish to be loved? Then love. If you abide by this simple principle, you should do well in marriage.

G for Grow in Grace

"For the unbelieving husband has been sanctified through his wife, and the unbelieving wife has been sanctified through her believing husband. Otherwise your children would be unclean, but as it is, they are holy" (1 Corinthians 7:14).

WHEN I ORIGINALLY DID MY STUDY on the seventh chapter of Corinthians in 2012, this verse really stuck out to me. I don't know how I could express my thought better, so I feel a need to quote what I wrote then:

Now Paul makes a remarkable statement that is not repeated anywhere else in any other form. He says that by virtue of the anointing and grace on the believing spouse, their significant other is sanctified (made clean), and so their children will be clean also. Everywhere else, we are taught that it is a personal relationship, that our faith cannot save anyone but ourselves. And even still, we are warned repeatedly of the dangers of such unholy unions (consider Solomon, brought to nought by his many affiliations). By this proclamation, Paul illustrates the exceeding grace God provides in our weakness when we believe (2 Cor 12:9). Because it is harder to keep the faith living in the midst of unbelievers, God has poured out even more grace – to overflowing – to the household of a believer, who converts in the midst of opposition (risking all, their spouse and children) to follow Him. So, though they lose it by forsaking it for God, they gain it back by its sanctification. This grace was not available before Jesus (John 1:17).

Paul isn't saying that there is greater grace available to Believers who go against godly wisdom to marry unbelievers. These have made their bed of coals and have only the assurance of torment (Isaiah 50:11). This greater grace is given for those who, in the midst of opposition from their unbelieving spouse, with the fear of rejection, believe in Jesus and choose to honour Him with their lives. Actually, I was wrong about the originality of this statement. Paul's response to the jailer, to "*...believe in the Lord Jesus and you will be saved, you and your household*" (Acts 16:31), also seems to convey this message of grace.

In this chapter, we will look at the grace that is available to believers in marriage, what it means to be gracious, and why we must be **as gracious as God** if we are going to make it until death do us part. The first thing we need to know is that there is already GRACE from God to handle the gift of marriage to His glory. Even if we were unbelievers when we married, our marriage is blessed, as we've already seen in B for Blessed to Bless, because it is a tool of God to teach the world about His great love. Even if you had no clue what love is before you married...if you are to succeed in marriage, you must certainly learn what love is; and in this process God ministers to all people.

However, God adds grace to His children to be victorious

in this mission. And to those who come to Him while already married, He gives them greater grace to stand and be a light unto their spouses and children. They don't have to forsake their marriages because they now believe in God. They can see themselves as His ministers in their marriage, who love their unbelieving spouse with the passion shown them by God while still in unbelief. Now, they too can have the great expectation, laid on God, that their marriage will succeed because His grace is sufficient for them in their weakness (2 Cor 12:9), and His love conquers all (1 Cor 13:8).

Now that God has given grace enough for both circumstances (two believers in marriage; a believer and an unbelieving spouse), we ought to also use the grace available to us and generously pass on the grace to our spouse. One would expect that a marriage between two believers would be easier and free from strife, as both would be gracious, having little to disagree on. But there is a problem of complacency that besets the affluent, which can also arise in marriage with two believers.

We tend to be more presumptuous of other believers, entitled and even judgmental, because *they should know better!* We may forget how much grace we have received from God and how much we are reliant on Him just to make it through a day. Like Jesus said, those who have been forgiven little, love little... (Luke 7:47). But it's not truly that you have been forgiven little, it is simply that you lose sight of (or don't even realise) how much you have been (and continue to be) forgiven.

Those who are faced with the reality of sin and human weakness constantly acknowledge the grace of God in their lives and are far more gracious to others. It is easier for them to reason that *they know not what they do* when offences arise. So, it is possible that in a household with only one believer, the believer would be more gracious to their unbelieving spouse because they are constantly reminded of the grace they enjoy in Christ. This also is the grace of God so that the unbeliever may come to know His love through their spouse.

Because a marriage is blessed does not guarantee its success. The addition of grace will help us to persevere and to do what is needful to make our marriage work...but it also doesn't guarantee its success. **We must choose to utilise the grace given and give grace as generously as we have received it from God, and His grace will continue to be poured out on our marriage and enable us to be victorious in this vocation.** If we are ungracious to our spouse, we work against God, and we work against ourselves.

So, what does it mean to be gracious? What does graciousness look like, and what is it not? The best model for grace is God Himself. He has shown us what grace is and what grace is not, and we ought to imitate Him if we want to excel in marriage.

> **1. Grace is Forgiving.** When people think about grace, they usually first think of forgiveness. And yes, a gracious person is a forgiving person. But forgiveness is simply one of the traits of a gracious person. A gracious person does not only forgive but forgives continually. They don't keep record of wrongs. They are also prone to forget offences because they never dwell on them. They cast them out quickly because, being wise, they know that meditating on wrongs suffered can only bear bad fruit (anger and bitterness being chief).
>
> **2. Grace is Understanding.** Those who are gracious are also self-aware. They know that they are not faultless themselves, and they appreciate the struggles we all face in the flesh and the empowerment the Holy Spirit gives to overcome sin. So, they are understanding of others who fall or struggle with sin, and rather than judge or accuse them, they stoop down to pick them up, wash them clean, and encourage and inspire them to good

works. They are not petty. They know when to make an issue of something and when to let a matter go. They are not easily offended. They are not contentious, like those who think they know it all and are the enforcers of righteousness.

3. Grace is Empathising. Gracious people easily empathise with the sufferings of others and are compassionate. They make room for the weakness of others, putting themselves in their position so as to make a righteous judgment. They are not critical but look for ways to uplift and enlighten the paths of those in darkness with godly wisdom. They choose their words carefully, knowing the power of words to build up or to tear down. They are patient, long-suffering, and hopeful, trusting that God works out all things to the good of those who love Him and are called according to His purpose (Rom 8:28).

4. Grace is Empowering. Gracious people love to celebrate others, so they are always looking for opportunities to help others to shine. They are kind and not envious of others. They are generous with compliments and praise, knowing that praise does more to encourage good behaviour than rebuke. They are also pre-emptive, so they are careful not to lay offences or stumbling blocks in the way of others, ensuring that they are more likely to overcome natural and unforeseen obstacles and grow spiritually. They are selfless, seeing themselves as a tool in God's hands to bless others.

5. Grace is Humbling. Ultimately, those who are gracious are humble. Through their gracious acts, they are continually humbled, as they are constantly aware of the spiritual battle for the souls of men and the many things that hinder people from coming to God and growing in His grace. They are very reliant on God to continue to be gracious and not to become complacent or self-righteous about all their goodness. The humbler they are, the more gracious they will be. And they will continue to grow in grace and humility.

Reading the above, would you consider yourself to be gracious? Would your spouse consider you to be gracious? What about your family and friends and colleagues? Grace emits into every aspect of our lives as we are becoming more like God each day we abide in grace and give grace to others. If those close to you don't see you as gracious, it is likely that you are not. You need to come to a renewed awareness of how much you have been forgiven, so that you will begin to love that much. Remember the new commandment: "*As I have loved you, love one another*" (John 13:34).

While we all need to make more effort to be gracious, we need to be careful not to abuse grace. Grace is abused when we see it as a license to sin or we excuse sin in others, without seeking to address it in a loving way. Grace is not afraid of confrontation, but it is empowered of God and guided by God to challenge sin and correct offenders in love. Being gracious doesn't mean everyone is our friend either, it just means that "...*if it is possible, as far as it depends on you, live at peace with everyone*" (Rom 12:18). You won't be liked or loved by everyone for being gracious. Just look at our shining example in Jesus Christ!

Offences are sure to come in your marriage, whether knowingly or unknowingly, accidental or incidental. You will have disagreements; big, small, and petty. But it takes only one gracious person to change the outcome of any interference. One gracious person can end an argument. One gracious person can restore a fallen spouse. One gracious person can influence the other to grow and walk in love.

Contrary to popular opinion, it doesn't take two people to make a marriage work. You don't have to give up on your marriage because you are putting in more than you are getting out. If you are married to an unbeliever, or your 'Christian' spouse is acting like an unbeliever, don't give up on your marriage thinking that it is hopeless. God has given grace enough. Trust Him and draw your strength from Him because He is with you. Remember, as long as the unbeliever is willing to abide in the marriage, there is grace enough (1 Cor 7:12-16) and hope that they will be saved (or restored) and the marriage will survive.

However, a far better marriage, with a greater likelihood of success, is where both are working together for the good of their union, building on a foundation of love. A sweet and beautiful marriage is one where both partners are as gracious as each other and striving to be as gracious as God. Such a marriage is possible when each makes a commitment and a daily decision to walk in the grace that God has abundantly provided for their blessed union.

Don't bank on your spouse being the gracious one. Don't wait to give tit for tat. Don't expect them to meet you halfway. Choose to be the gracious one yourself, and give 100%, and who knows if you won't soon be enjoying the sweetest marriage ever known to man!

H for Honesty is the Best Policy

I THINK IT WAS BENJAMIN FRANKLIN who said "*Honesty is the best policy...*" (REF 4d), and I would have to agree. Many people feel that there must be an exception, as it seems that to every rule there is an exception. They suppose that it is not always wise or kind to be totally honest and argue that it is not always possible to be totally honest either. Some even say, "*be honest about your dishonesty,*" because of this belief that absolute truthfulness is not only impossible but foolish.

There seems to be some wisdom in this reasoning that honesty may not always be the best policy. There appears to be wisdom in the saying that "*what they don't know won't hurt them...*" There appears to be some wisdom in the counsel that "*telling him/her the truth now will only make YOU feel better, but it will make matters worse.*" But again, I have to agree with

Thomas Jefferson who is credited with the saying, "*Honesty is the first chapter in the book of wisdom*" (REF 4e). Also, Jesus, the wisest of all, said, "**the Truth will set you free**" (John 8:32).

So, however wise or kind or loving it may feel to think that some deception, some lies, some half-truths is necessary to keep the peace...don't believe it! **The Truth is a powerful Redeemer! Even if it offends you, even if it hurts you, even if it breaks you...it will heal you and restore your relationship, and set you free from captivity to the enemy of your soul - "the father of lies"** (John 8:44)!

As Christians, we cannot accept any other policy for intimacy in our marriages. Honesty is the best and only policy. In the absence of honesty, there can be no intimacy. There can be no trust, and as such, there can be no relationship. We should be wary of accepting worldly wisdom, which appears to be wise but is just foolishness. The truth will hurt, it may even kill you...but within it is resurrection power. Remember, "*do not be afraid of those who kill the body but cannot kill the soul. Instead, fear the One who can destroy both soul and body in hell*" (Matt 10:28).

For us to be honest with others, we need to first be honest with ourselves. If we are not being truthful to ourselves, we have no hope of being honest with others. We may begin to apologise but still justify our actions. We may say we are sorry but still blame them or someone else for our mistake. We may say we accept responsibility, and own up to everything we did wrong but still tell ourselves that we were not as bad as all that, and we only confessed for their benefit. No, we need to strip it all down before God and see the truth about ourselves clearly if we are to sincerely confess and repent of our error.

When it comes to confessing your sin to others, it is best not to overthink it. If you do so, you may want to pad up the truth with lies to make it easier to swallow. Or you might even deceive the person by allowing room for misunderstanding so that you are essentially off the hook - because you did tell them the truth, but they thought you meant something else. It is best to come right out with it. After you have owned up to your error and confronted your dishonesty - speak the truth, owning your fault. Be sincere and humble.

The Bible says, "*a broken and a contrite heart, O God, You will not despise*" (Psalm 51:17). If it is good enough for God, it is good enough for men. When you are broken by the truth and confess your sins to your spouse, they will know that God has forgiven you, and they will be compelled to do the same...because if they do not forgive, they know that they will not be forgiven (Matt 6:15).

Yes, it may take time... They may still be angry and want to vent. Allow them. Don't run from the consequences of your actions. Face the music.

But what if the issue is not about your fault...what if they are at fault, and you want to confront them about it? What if it isn't a matter of who is at fault and just a difference of opinion on an issue? You may wonder if conceding on a disagreement is being dishonest. Or if it would be dishonest to not thrash out every issue when addressing sin in your spouse. This is where applying love and wisdom comes in. Be brutally honest about your faults, but be gentle and tactful with others.

Why the difference? Because you are not God who knows all things, and you may very well be wrong in your assessment. You must always give them the benefit of the doubt and not take on the role of the Holy Spirit in your spouse's life, by trying to *convict* them of sin.

When you have brought up the issue, speaking the truth in love, pray and trust the Holy Spirit to work in them, to bring them to humility and submission to the truth... And when He does, they will come to you freely, broken and contrite, to lay all things bare. But if you wrestle with them to be as brutally honest as you have been with them, you may simply cause them to hide more for fear of your judgment and rejection. Persevere to show them, through your example and unconditional positive regard, the way of truth and love.

If you are both Christians, who are led by the Spirit of God, your relationship should be characterised by:

1. Humility. Humility is essentially being honest with yourself. You can't be humble unless you are honest with yourself. You will see yourself the way God sees you, and you will be convicted of sin and will confess your faults, even without others pointing it out. If you are humble, you won't be quick to judge others, but you will be gracious towards them and pray for God to lead them to the knowledge of the truth. You will be ready and quick to forgive and restore others when they come for forgiveness and healing.

2. Sincerity. Sincerity is an attitude of truthfulness that abides with an honest person. A sincere person is open and free from deceit. They speak the truth with ease, without needing to think of how to present it to others, even when they know that it would hurt. If they are also humble, their words will always be filled with grace towards others so that, though their words convict, they never sting.

3. Honesty. Honesty is the absence of deception. A relationship that is characterised by honesty is one where BOTH are humble and sincere. They are open and free with each other, and this makes room for trust to grow.

4. Trust. Trust is a seed that only grows in a haven of honesty. As the sincerity of both are tested overtime, their trust in each other grows. It is not easily broken where there is a firm character of humility and sincerity already established. Even if one was to falter, trust may wane, but with the entrance of truth, it will stand strong again.

5. Peace. This is the sweet fruit of a relationship where trust grows and abides. You will never need to second guess your spouse. You won't need to question them on their behaviour. You will KNOW them, in the deepest and truest way. You will have real intimacy, and because you trust them completely, you do not keep anything hidden from them either. And you will be KNOWN, understood, and appreciated for all that you are.

If you allow dishonesty to thrive in your relationship, you will never experience this kind of peace and intimacy. Your relationship will be infected with distrust and will crumble at the slightest infraction. If you personally lack humility and/or sincerity, you have *little* hope of establishing honesty in your marriage. Even if your spouse is humble and sincere, your insincerity will remain a hindrance to growth in trust and intimacy in your relationship.

Your secrets will become your bedfellows, and they will widen the gap between you and your spouse. First spiritually, then emotionally, mentally, and ultimately, physically. They will become your burden, your curse, and your nightmare! Don't give place to the enemy (Eph 4:27). Honesty *is* the best policy!

I for Intimacy

"And they were both naked, the man and his wife, and were not ashamed" (Genesis 2:25).

WHEN MOST PEOPLE THINK of intimacy, they generally think about sexual intimacy, but intimacy is about much more than sex. There are several ways to be intimate with your spouse, and physical intimacy (which includes sexual intercourse) is just one. A healthy and strong marriage is one in which you are intimate in EVERY way with your spouse. Then you really are as ONE and no longer two, which is God's intention for every marriage (Gen 2:24).

So, intimacy is not another word for sex, nor is it another word for love. You can love someone without being intimate with them, and you can have sex with someone without intimacy. But can you be intimate with someone you do not love? What is intimacy?

If I may give it a try, I would say, "***intimacy means***

having deep knowledge, understanding, and affection for someone with whom you have a close relationship, where you are also known, understood, and loved deeply." Intimacy is mutual, it is not a one-sided affair. It requires a commitment to the other person, based on a recognition of your love and need for each other.

In my post, **Intimacy with God**, I wrote about how God loves the whole world but is intimate with a chosen few. They are the ones who have also made a commitment to love Him and enter into a close relationship with Him. The deepest form of intimacy between two people is seen in the marriage relationship, which is consummated through the act of sexual intercourse. When two people are intimate in every other way and come together sexually, they are vulnerable and submitted to each other, and their sexual activity is more than sex; it is intimacy expressed physically.

However, some marriages rely on sex alone, without developing true intimacy by seeking to know and be known. And where there is a lack of intimacy in other areas, perhaps by a refusal to communicate (or communicate honestly), or refusing to make time for each other (and other forms of negligence), even their sexual activity declines because of their lack of emotional connection. Having an active sex life does not guarantee an intimately healthy marriage. However, if you are intimate in other ways, you will also grow in physical intimacy, and your sexual activity will receive a boost.

So, what are these other ways to nurture and express intimacy in marriage? Drawing from an article by Tony & Alisa, on **"6 Forms of Intimacy to Building A Strong Marriage"** (REF 2a), we have:

> **1. Emotional Intimacy.** This is paramount for a healthy, loving relationship. We are emotional beings and have emotional needs as powerful as our physical needs for food and water. We long to belong, to be understood, and to be cherished. If we are not able to meet this need

for an emotional connection with our spouse, we become vulnerable to infidelity, as we seek to meet the need elsewhere, or respond in desperation to someone else who takes the time to connect with us emotionally. That is why the Bible says, *"Guard your heart with all diligence, for out of it come the issues of life…"* (Prov 4:23). We need to make time to talk about our feelings, fears, and desires with our spouse so that we can be emotionally vulnerable with them, understood in the deepest way.

2. Intellectual Intimacy. You will be surprised at the number of affairs that begin on this level of connection. In addition to our emotional needs, we have mental and intellectual needs. We are attracted to people we admire intellectually, who challenge our thinking or who inspire us intellectually. We respect such people and feel proud to be associated with them. But even though we may have intellectual connections with our colleagues or associates at work, we need to maintain a deep intellectual intimacy with our spouse, which means that we are able to talk to them about any and everything…and we actually enjoy such discussions.

3. Spiritual Intimacy. As spiritual beings, we need to be in agreement with our spouse spiritually. If we are not, we will not be able to grow in intimacy with them. We will have conflicting interests, desires, beliefs, and attitudes that will challenge our ability to respect, appreciate, and understand each other. And when there is a disconnect here, our emotional and intellectual connections are weakened. But if we are able to connect with our spouse on this level, the road to deeper intimacy is clear because we will have inner peace with ourselves and each other. Make sure you spend time to nurture your spiritual connection and build each other up spiritually. And if you are Christian and not yet married, remember that you should not seek to be joined with an unbeliever (2 Cor 6:14).

4. Recreational Intimacy. We are also social beings, and our lives are about more than our work. We need to make time to play. What activities make us happy? What makes us laugh? We need to know and share our interests with our spouse, then we can enjoy these activities together and grow to know, understand, and appreciate each other better. What you give your time to shows what you love, and who you spend your time with shows who you love. There will be some activities that you prefer to do alone, that you may be more efficient tackling alone, but be wary of doing too much on your own. You are a team now. Make time for and get used to doing things together, and you will soon find that you share the same favourite things, and you are inseparable!

5. Financial Intimacy. Money matters greatly in a relationship, and how you spend your money also matters. Do you both have the same values when it comes to money? Is one a big spender and the other a miser? Is one an investor while the other thinks only of today? Are you open about your financial needs, spending habits, and ambitions? Or do you live independently of each other financially, not knowing nor caring about each other's financial needs, habits, and goals?

You might think it is a moot point, but there is a reason Jesus said, "*...where your treasure is, there your heart will be also*" (Matt 6:21). If you are being secretive about your finances or think it is personal and private and not any of your spouse's business, you are keeping your heart from them and keeping yourself from being vulnerable with them. You have to lay it all down and know that what you have is theirs; your loss is their loss, your gain is their gain, and vice versa. You are a team, so make sure you are transparent in this regard too, and ensure that you agree for the sake of your relationship and your dependents.

Now, if you are connected on all these levels, there really is nothing standing in the way of your physical intimacy. Physical intimacy is, however, more than sex. It includes all forms of touches, caresses, kissing, playing, cuddling, and love making. It also requires faithfulness to one another.

Can you imagine being sexually intimate with someone who you know is unfaithful to you? Or who you suspect is or has been unfaithful to you? You may be able to have sex, but this breakdown of trust will greatly limit your physical intimacy.

If you are looking to grow intimacy in your marriage, these are the five steps to achieving a deeper connection with your spouse:

> **1. Agreement and Acceptance.** I've quoted this once or twice already, but it is essentially important to this topic. The Bible asks, *"can two walk together unless they agree?"* (Amos 3:3). The first barrier to intimacy with your spouse is disagreement. If your home is filled with conflict, tension, and misunderstanding, how can you grow in appreciation of one another? It is best to think about and settle on this before you marry, and make sure that the person you choose agrees with you in the five areas of intimacy above – as much as is reasonably possible. If there is a disconnect, you may find yourself being secretive, or avoiding discussions so that you won't argue, or living independently for lack of mutual interest or, even worse, respect.
>
> However, as we saw under C for Communicate Effectively, we may never have 100% agreement. That is where it is important for us to know, appreciate, and

accept our differences as a couple, as male and female. Culturally, socially, emotionally, physically, intellectually, spiritually, and financially, we need to know what we are willing to accept and make an informed decision to marry them. If after the wedding, we realise that we didn't cover all our bases, and things are not as we thought, we must still accept our spouse as our choice and work towards agreement, by humbling ourselves and walking in love.

2. Transparency and Vulnerability. As we learnt from H for Honesty is the Best Policy, secrecy is the enemy of intimacy. Where there is secrecy, there is no trust, and there will be no understanding and peace. Rather, there will be fear, anxiety, suspicion, resentment, and everything that will stifle love. It is important for intimacy for you to be transparent with each other, open and honest with all things, so that you will fully be known, understood, and appreciated for all that you are.

When you open yourself to your spouse in this way, you allow yourself to be vulnerable, allowing them to see your weaknesses and flaws... And when you are loved, flaws and all, it is the deepest connection you can have with another human being. It is the truest form of acceptance, which is what we all crave...to be loved just as we are. But if you pretend, and you are loved, you won't enjoy intimacy because you won't believe that you are truly loved...and you would be right, because the person they think they love is not you! So, you will be insecure and afraid of being found out for who you really are, and ultimately rejected. This fear is like a self-fulfilling prophecy; it keeps you from knowing and being loved. But we know that "*there is no fear in love; but perfect love casteth out fear: because fear hath torment. He that feareth is not made perfect in love*" (1 John 4:18).

3. Service and Submission. "*My little children, let us not* *love in word, neither in tongue; but in deed and in truth*" (1 John 3:18). It is a farce to talk of love and not to show it in the way we serve one another, in the way we submit to one another. Such love is as vain as faith without works (Jam 2:14-26). Anyone who truly loves is compelled to show it by their actions, and not only compelled, they *desire* to show it. If this instinct has not arisen in us, we can stir it up and stimulate it by intentionally doing good to our spouse, looking for opportunities to serve them in love and submitting to them, by smashing our pride, going the extra mile, and the other ways we learnt in D for Die Daily to Self. We can and should develop a habit of serving, as we seek to bless each other, and thus nurture our marriage to bear fruit, as we learnt in B for Blessed to Bless.

4. Friendship and Fellowship. Friendship is the bedrock of every marriage. It is built on agreement, acceptance, respect, and mutual affection. Before two can be one, before they can be lovers, they must be friends. We looked into this in F for Friends Forever. Nurturing your friendship is important for keeping your marriage on a strong foundation. Even when the romantic feelings fade, you can stand on your friendship as a platform to rediscover your feelings of love again.

It has been said that "*a successful marriage requires falling in love many times, always with the same person*" (Mignon McLaughlin, REF 4f). Be ready to fight for your love. Friendship is best nurtured in marriage by fellowship. You need to MAKE time for and spend time with each other, do things together, and share everything equally, working together to achieve your hopes and dreams.

5. Appreciation and Adoration. Complacency can set in if we do not watch out for it and resist it. If that happens, one or both partners will begin to feel unappreciated and unloved. You need to counter that by intentionally appreciating your spouse for who they are and their partnership and contribution to your life. This was the first topic we looked at in A for Appreciation. Those who are appreciated are motivated to respond with affection. So, by appreciating your spouse, you are actually increasing their capacity to love. And don't stop at appreciation...move on to adoration! Yes, shower your spouse with love. Be affectionate. Be romantic. Be attentive. Be present. You want to love with wild abandon, and they want to be loved with wild abandon, so let go, and do it. They too want to love with wild abandon, and you want to be loved with wild abandon, so let them...

Learn from the five love languages we looked at in C for Communicate Effectively, and discover which language your spouse speaks and understands best. Speak their love language. Do nice and thoughtful things for your spouse to let them know they are loved. Enjoy your marriage as God intended.

If you follow these five steps, you are sure to fall in love over and over again with your spouse and enjoy the deepest intimacy possible between two people. It takes sincerity and work to keep intimacy in your marriage. You have to be honest with yourself about the level of intimacy in your marriage and where there is a lack so you can do the needed work to make it up. Don't settle for an okay marriage when you can have a wonderful marriage with a little more effort and consideration. Intimacy is its own reward. In time, you will be glad you made the effort.

J for JOY!

THE WEDDING DAY IS RIGHTFULLY a most joyous day, as a community of friends and family come together to celebrate the sacred union of two of their own, in love and in marriage. At that time, the great potential of marriage is celebrated, as the two lovebirds are sent on the voyage of love in the ocean called "Marriage". Their hearts are filled with joy and hope and faith and love... With the greatness of their love, they believe that they can conquer any obstacles that may come their way, and they are eager to start on their adventure.

Sadly, this feeling of joy, hope, faith, and love seems to die down as they progress along the ocean of marriage. As they face the rough seas and cold nights...their love and faith are tested...and their joy meets frustration, and hope meets depression. They begin to wonder if they have what it takes after all... They wonder if their wedding day would be the height of their joy...or if, in fact, such joy can be relived and even surpassed in their marriage.

The truth is that our joy in any endeavour in this life is not tied to the endeavour itself, but to our purpose. If we lose sight of our purpose, we lose the savour of joy. When you lose joy, you go in search of it through *enjoyment* and have momentary periods of happiness, which, when they pass, often leave you with *depression,* causing you to repeat the search for joy; yet lasting joy evades you. **But when we retain a sense of purpose, we see meaning even in suffering (Jam 1:2-4), and we have hope and are able to abide in joy, having faith in God who gave us a purposeful existence.**

The joy in marriage is tied to the *purpose* for which marriage was created. Marriage, itself, has no joy. A marriage that is entered into wrongly, which is not submitted to the law of God, offers no joy to those who engage in it. It is in fact a burden and a bondage to those submitted to it. It will be as effective in accomplishing the will of God as the Law was effective in making man righteous...

God gives marriage purpose, and He is the source of joy within marriage. As we saw in B for Blessed to Bless, a primary purpose of marriage is to teach us about the enduring love of God and to minister this love to the world. Our connection to Him and recognition of Him as the centre will enable us to find and retain joy in marriage. However, if we take Him out of the equation and trust in our own way, we can only expect a disaster as we find that our love is unable to endure all things... We may enjoy brief or even long moments of happiness, but joy will ultimately evade us because joy originates from and is sustained by God.

Well, someone might say, even Christian marriages, where Christ is upheld as centre, are lacking in joy, and many end up in divorce. This is true. Jesus said, "*according to your faith will it be done to you*" (Matt 9:29). Many Christian marriages are so in theory alone, not in practice. Many people do not show by their actions that they believe the things they profess with their mouths, so their works reveal the truth of their faith (Jam 2:14-26). If their faith is dead by works, how can their marriages show forth the power of God?

So, we see that we too have a part to play in unleashing the power of God in our marriage. We have to show our faith in Him by our works of love and submission - first to Him, then to each other. When we act as His agents, we act according to His purpose for our marriage, and we will be successful, and we will have the joy we truly desire. The link between purpose and joy cannot be overstated. We should all know that we are happiest when we do what we are created to do…when we are walking in the will of God, fully exercising the potential He has hid in us.

Here are five things we can and should be doing to retain and grow our experience of joy in marriage:

1. Nurture our Relationship. We should do this by paying attention to each other, spending time with each other, communicating truthfully, and growing in intimacy. We must build on the foundation of friendship and work to keep romance in the relationship, by communicating in each other's preferred love language. We must also serve one another in love, submitting to one another and lifting each other up.

2. Cherish our Gift. We must appreciate each other and treasure the covenant of marriage. We must protect our marriage from external influences by being on guard against temptation, complacency, pride, dishonesty, and other roots of discord that wish to destroy our holy bond. We should develop the habit of speaking life into our relationship, through regular prayer and kind words of affirmation, and not speaking death, either by bad-mouthing our spouse or thinking bad about our spouse.

3. Mature in Christ. We should grow in our walk with Christ, such that He moulds us daily into His likeness.

We should begin to exhibit the fruit of the Spirit, being "...*love, joy, peace, forbearance, kindness, goodness, faithfulness, gentleness, and self-control*" (Gal 5:22-23). Our lives should be disciplined and fruitful. And as we grow in graciousness, we are more able to live in peace and love with our spouse.

4. Endure through Trials. When we are mature in Christ, we are able to endure trials, knowing that they build up our character (Rom 5:3-5), and knowing also that Christ, who is with us, will bring us out of every trial with testimonies (Rom 8:28)! In the midst of a trial, we continue to do what is right and do not fall for the lies of the enemy to turn us away from faith and faithfulness. Trials are for a reason and for a season and must be endured by keeping our eyes on God.

5. Trust in God. As we keep our eyes on God, our faith will not fail us, neither will our love run cold because our expectation is not laid in man, but in God. When we have done everything else, all that remains for us to do is to stand (Eph 6:13). We must trust God, the Author and Finisher of our Faith, to honour His own name, carry us through, and bring us out victorious (Heb 12:2; 1 Cor 10:13). We know that He is love, and He never fails. Has God not promised? He will surely show Himself faithful (Num 23:19; 2 Tim 2:13).

So, my brothers and sisters, the joy of marriage is yours for the taking. It comes with the correct and faithful exercise of your gift, marriage. Joy is God's promise to the righteous (Prov 10:28), so don't let the lies of the enemy cause you to forsake the path of faith and faithfulness. God never promised you that the road would be easy...only that it will end in pure joy if you will trust and obey every step of the way. Also remember that joy is not simply the reward for completion. As you abide in Him, He will sustain you with joy through the whole journey.

K for Kiss and Keep Kissing

SOMEONE ONCE SAID "*KISSING is one of the best kept secrets of 'happily ever after'*" (REF 4g), and I can't help but agree.

I know the obvious word for this week's letter, K, would have been 'Kindness,' but I didn't want to go with the obvious. And I honestly think I have said PLENTY about being kind and loving to your spouse so far in this series. So, not to keep repeating myself, I decided to look at this fascinating activity called 'kissing.'

Why do we kiss? Well, the definition of kiss given by Google seems to answer that for us. It says a kiss is a *"touch or caress with the lips as a sign of love, sexual desire, or greeting"* (REF 3). So, we kiss to show someone that they are loved, not necessarily to express sexual interest (as in the case of kissing between friends and family members). We also kiss to indicate our interest in sexual activity and our sexual attraction to the other person. Or we can simply kiss as an indication of acceptance, as in a greeting (not necessarily to someone we know and love).

Kisses tend to have cultural significance, and in some cultures, people habitually kiss strangers, so a kiss is not much of a big deal. In others, kissing is seen only as an expression of sexual interest, so these people may not kiss as a greeting or even as an expression of love to family. Based on the culture you grew up in, you may be a free kisser or a shy kisser. Two different people with their diverse cultural experiences of kissing will bring different interpretations and expectations of kissing into their marriage.

It is good to know ourselves, and it paramount that we know our spouse and what communicates love to them. If they love kissing a lot, and you don't fancy it much, who should adjust? Should they be denied this avenue to express their love because you don't feel like it?

It is a form of communication, just like talking, and it doesn't help to shut it down because we don't feel like it. We have to make the effort to communicate love in a way that it will be understood and appreciated. So just as the shy talker needs to make more effort to speak up and engage, the shy kisser needs to take more initiative in expressing love through kissing.

Moreover, kissing is not simply an expression of love, acceptance, or sexual interest. **Kissing is a CELEBRATION of love! Every time you kiss your spouse, you are celebrating the love that you have for each other, not simply communicating it.** Your love is special, not like any other. Your relationship is special because there is no one you can kiss with the intimacy and passion that you can and should kiss your spouse. Kissing is you delighting in your spouse and in the knowledge that you are his, and she is yours (and vice versa).

Also, as a sign of affection, kissing is an investment in your relationship. No kiss you give your spouse is ever wasted. Kisses are like little pennies that fill up a piggy bank. The more you kiss your spouse, the more affectionate they grow towards you. You fill their love up! Likewise, the less you kiss your spouse, the less affectionate they will be towards you.

Kissing breaks down barriers. It softens a tense situation by reminding the person that your love is still present, and that is the most important thing. Kisses heal hurting hearts. They serve as an affirmation that the person is cherished and desired. Many marriages would be saved if couples would intentionally make the effort to kiss each other genuinely and kiss each other often.

So Kissing is:

1. A message of acceptance;

2. An expression of love;

3. A solicitation for sexual intimacy;

4. A celebration of your relationship;

5. An investment of affection.

Kisses are powerful in binding, mending, and growing affection between couples. They shouldn't be abused and used for covering up deceit in one's heart (the way Judas betrayed Jesus). They shouldn't be abused and used to circumvent an issue, such that you never actually talk about the issue but bury it under kisses. Kisses shouldn't be abused and used as the ONLY means of expression of love. There are many other ways to show love…so while doing the others, don't neglect to KISS intentionally, spontaneously, passionately, and regularly. And while kissing, don't neglect the others…

The powers of kissing work best when the foundation of friendship, love, and intimacy have been laid. Kisses with kindness, humility, and respect, will go a long way to build intimacy, where there is already a foundation of friendship in marriage. If kissing is not your thing, begin to kiss dutifully until it becomes habitual, and it will soon become an essential and joyous release of the affection that has been growing inside of you for your spouse. That's the magic of kissing.

IS IT OKAY TO KISS WHILE DATING?

I was asked this question by a reader of my blog once, and my answer got me in quite a bit of trouble. But it also taught me lessons about myself, what is holy, and what is right.

I think we have already acknowledged that kissing is a largely cultural phenomenon. It is also a mode of communication, and a whole lot can be communicated through a kiss…including sexual desire. We've also seen that kissing is a stimulant. It stirs up affection and a desire for sexual intimacy. If you're dating and wish to abstain from sex before marriage, kissing would be unwise for you, though it may be culturally acceptable, even by other professing Believers.

Kissing while dating might seem like a simple, harmless expression of one's feelings. It may feel natural, right, good, and normal to us. Some Christians might even say it aids abstinence because you have an outlet for your *natural* desire. You don't have to go 'cold turkey' and be 'Mother Theresa' or 'Saint Francis.' It's all about self-control…

Honestly, this was my thinking when I initially answered the enquirer.

But a friend of mine got me to look deeper and consider what is going on spiritually. You have to ask yourself what's on your mind as you kiss or entice another person? Are your hands, your body, and your mind lusting for more? Is kissing helping you to focus on your spiritual or illicit carnal needs? Also, what about the other person?

Do you really know how the person you are kissing is coping with it? Are you sure of the message they are receiving from your kiss? Do you care that your kisses may be stimulating their desire to fornicate with you - or with someone else? Maybe they are not as strong as you are. Our desire, as Believers, should always be to walk in wisdom and love, so we must be careful not to act in a way that would cause others to stumble.

Also, there is a saying; "*prevention is better than cure*" (REF 4h). If you stimulate your sexual desire through kisses, you'd eventually need sexual intercourse or masturbation to put out the fire of your passion. But as a cure, these are quite pathetic because they are so insatiable, and they create new problems for the single person.

Consequently, you would need to keep having pre-marital sex or end the relationship because of the risks it presents to you and your desire for righteousness. However, by then, you would have hurt both yourself and your special friend. That was why Solomon advised the daughters of Jerusalem to "*...not stir up love until it pleases...*" (Songs 8:4 NKJV). Basically, wait until the appointed time and place, in marriage.

If we really think about it and sincerely search our hearts, we will know that, by kissing while dating and saying we want to wait till marriage for sex, we are playing with fire. We are deceiving ourselves. So, the Bible asks, "*can a man walk on hot coals without his feet being scorched?*" (Prov 6:28, NIV). The answer is obviously no.

Kissing is deeply powerful, as you would have gathered from this chapter, and like fire, it has a right place. It must not be abused. So, even if you see it happening in the movies, read about it in a novel, or even walk in on it in your living room, choose to walk in wisdom and love. Save your kiss, and honour your body as you wait to marry the one you love.

L for L.O.V.E

LOVE. HOW CAN YOU HAVE a discussion about marriage and not talk about love? It's impossible. There is also that issue of what definition of love...? What type/s of love is/are needed to make a marriage beautiful and successful?

We have talked much about love, so far. We have discussed various attributes of love, shown in selflessness, service, honesty, and affection. So far, I have presented a definition of love based on Christianity, which sees love as an act of the will, not a feeling. The greatest example we have for love is God Himself, and Jesus' sacrificial death on the Cross represents this great love God has for Mankind. We have seen that this is the type of love that ensures for a blessed, beautiful, and successful marriage.

But is the emotional component of love irrelevant? Most of the time, when people talk of love and think about love, they are talking about an emotional state of being. Loving music, for example, is not an act of the will. Loving ice-cream has nothing to do with choosing to be loving towards ice-cream! We just go "oooh, ahhh" whenever we see ice cream, and we never have to try to enjoy it. It just sort of comes naturally. It is the way it makes us feel, like Ronan Keating sings.

For most people...this is love, and this is the love that matters to them. This is the love that *moves* them to ACT in Christian love. Because they have these wonderful feelings towards somebody else, they *instinctively* desire their happiness, they want to serve them. They act kindly towards them and consider their lover's needs above their own. And when the feelings subside, and they no longer instinctively want to please the other person, they say they no longer love them, and they start looking for someone else who they can live for and delight in.

This is the romantic love that is all too important at the start of a relationship. It is a kick starter, a launcher, allowing you to do the impossible, without considering the cost to self or pride. It is passionate and fierce. It is sexually charged. It is also unfortunately innately selfish. It revolves around how the person FEELS, so it is quite volatile. It is very emotional, taking the bearer of this love from one extreme of adoration and appreciation of life to another extreme of depression and hatred of life (if the feelings are not mutual).

Can you really build a marriage on something so fickle? Evidence shows that you cannot. Many marriages reliant on only romantic love as their bind soon collapse under the weight of reality. But the presence of this type of love makes it easier to act out the God-kind of love. You can see it as an essential ingredient in marriage, like the oil of an engine. It just makes everything work easier and better together, without friction. The secret is how to keep this passionate love alive and mutual through the long-haul of marriage.

Least of all, there ought to be brotherly love between spouses, which is genuine affection and respect for the other person; what we owe to all our fellow humans. Having brotherly love shows that we are not selfish, we are considerate, we are kind, we are friendly. Brotherly love may not have the enduring power of Christ's love, nor the passion of romantic love, but most marriages can survive with just this love present.

The marriage may survive, but it may not be happy. Without any major crisis, without temptations or strife, you can pretty much live in peace with someone else, who you respect and have genuine affection for, even if you do not have strong romantic feelings for them. But when strife comes, trouble brews, and temptations abound, you need Christ's sacrificial and enduring love to weather the storms and to keep doing right by your spouse, even if it hurts.

The Greeks had other names for these types of love and defined seven types of love. An article by Rania Naim (REF 2b) gives a good guide. They are:

1. Eros - Love of the Body (Sexual Attraction)

2. Philia - Love of the Mind (Friendship)

3. Ludus - Playful love (Infatuation)

4. Pragma - Longstanding love (Commitment)

5. Agape - Love of the Soul (Charity)

6. Philautia - Love of the Self (Self-love)

7. Storge - Love of the Child (Instinctive, Protective, and Sacrificial)

I am not proficient with the Greek definitions, but I am able to see that the God-kind of love or Christ-like love consists of Agape, Pragma, Philia, and Storge. Brotherly love consists of Philia and Agape. And romantic love consists of Eros, Philia, Ludus, and Philautia. A marriage needs every one of these types of love to be healthy and happy - yes, including and especially self-love. If you are unable to love yourself, how can you begin to love another?

We can see that brotherly love is fully contained in Christ-like love. Brotherly love answers to the commandments, "*love your neighbour as yourself*" (Mark 12:31) and "*do to others as you would have them do to you*" (Matt 7:12). It is a love we can give to anyone, which we are commanded to give to even our enemies (Matt 5:44).

Christ-like love includes the added elements of commitment and sacrifice, and it is a love we are expected to show to those in the Family of God, including our spouses. It answers to the new command which Christ gave to His disciples; "*as I have loved you, love one another*" (John 13:34). We can and should love all of God's people with this enduring, unconditional love.

It would suffice to love our spouses with the Christ-like love, which has brotherly love and *then some*. But we shouldn't downplay the importance and benefits of romantic love, even in Christian marriages. We don't have romantic love with our children, nor with our Christian brothers and sisters. But it is needful to have this emotional component in a marriage relationship if our marriages are to be blissful rather than a burdensome cross we bear.

I even suppose that there is an emotional element to the love Christ has for us, even if it isn't exactly romantic in the sexual sense. I don't think He came to die for us simply out of duty. I believe there was passion for us, emotion that compelled Him to orchestrate the romantic deliverance that was the Cross. It was not merely an act of the will, nor would I suppose that His love for us arose from His will or mind...but from His heart...and it became His will until on the Cross, His nature was revealed.

If you think about it, there's a strong emotional element to the love we have for our children, our close friends, and some family members. These feelings we have for them enhance our intimacy and interaction with them. It sets those relationships apart from the others.

Too many people deny the power of the heart, of passion or the emotional component in love, forgetting that this motivates and drives man even above his will. We must not undermine the role of emotions in the full expression of love. We shouldn't give it centre stage, but it must have its place. Our emotional needs in marriage must be met by not only showing brotherly love but romantic love to our spouse. Emotional affairs, which often lead to sexual infidelity, arise when this emotional component is missed or neglected in one or both spouses.

You can think of it this way. Romantic love is the love that says "I want you." Isn't it great to be wanted? Even God wants to be wanted, not simply needed. How would you like it if someone keeps telling you, "I need you, I need you," but they never say nor show that they want you? They always choose other things when it is convenient for them. They want other things, but they need you, so they are stuck with you and are cheating on you with the things they want... Or maybe they don't even need you but are simply enduring you...putting up with you or loving from pity or duty.

We would even prefer to hear "I want you, even though I don't need you."

With God, we should both want and need Him. However, we will always need Him, regardless of whether we want Him or not. But we can want our spouse, even if we don't need them. In fact, it is better that way at the beginning. And as we grow in love and understanding and compatibility and commitment, we will grow in mutual dependency, and we will both need and want them...even though our need for them will never be greater than our need for God, and we should never want them more than we want God.

I hope you are following me here.

I have harped on about Christ-like love from the beginning of this book, and I feel a need to harp on a little about romantic love, lest people think that such is only for fools or for the world. **Romantic love has an important role in our marriages, but the cornerstone and the foundation of Christ must be laid first, and romance can be the gems that adorn our marriage and make the experience of being married delightful.**

If romantic love was not important at all, then I suppose Christians should have arranged marriages with other Christians, who have been shown to be compatible with them in personality and purpose. They will be able to love each other as Christ loves the Church...as is their duty to love all of the people of God. Maybe many Christians already approach their marriages as a God set-up that has nothing to do with their emotions. But I don't think this is Biblical. Songs of Solomon is one book that celebrates the beauty of romance.

What we don't want to do is to be led by our emotions when deciding who to marry. It should be one of the things we consider, but of much better consideration are:

1. if the person belongs to the Family of God;

2. whether or not they are submitted to God; and

3. if you have genuine affection and respect for each other.

If you have this foundation, then enjoy romance, and let it remain grounded on the foundation of Christ. And it will adorn your marriage and will be preserved in your relationship by the staying power of Christ's enduring love.

It is true that "*a successful marriage requires falling in love many times, always with the same person*" – (Mignon McLaughlin, REF 4f). I think this requires being honest with ourselves about what we want out of life and marriage. If you are content not to have passion in your marriage and only desire a companion, then do enjoy your simplicity. However, consider your spouse. Do they desire a passionate, romantic love? Do they know that you are not emotionally, romantically, nor sexually invested in the relationship? You need to be truthful with them so that they do not feel cheated later.

If you are already married and want to rekindle the romantic feelings in your marriage, these five steps should help.

1. Sleep together. Don't simply have sex and get on with it. Intentionally fall asleep together in each other's arms. Make your bedtime special, for not only sexual intimacy but also emotional intimacy. Settle in for the night together, and spend time together alone in your room.

2. Date often. Make time regularly for each other to do things together out of the house, and occasionally, spend a romantic evening in together. Be intentional about it. But also allow room for some spontaneous outings. Invite each other to work events as well, so that even if you have to be away from your home, you can still be together.

3. Be affectionate. Increase your physical intimacy by touching and kissing often, cuddling, holding hands, and playing with each other. Engage in activities that require physical closeness, like going to the movies together, or going for walks, and even swimming! As your physical intimacy grows, your sexual desire for each other will also increase, and your intimacy in the bedroom will deepen.

4. Hang out with each other's friends. Social hang-outs allow you to see each other in a different way, and it also broadens your discussion topics. If you are always talking about the kids, hanging out with your friends together should bring you out of that cocoon. As you get to know and bond with your spouse's friends, you also learn more about their character and their likes and dislikes. Your shared interests and activities will also expand, as you go out for fun group outings.

5. Allow some personal space. It's great and important to do things together, but you should also allow time for yourself and give your spouse the time to do something they like that you may not be so interested in. Women may love a day at the spa. Men may love to play football with their friends. Time apart also allows you to miss one another and have more things to talk about when you come back together. But watch this. Your interests shouldn't be addictive and eat into the quality time you could be spending together.

With these five tips, I hope you will be able to rekindle the spark in your marriage. Even without the spark, as long as you have and show the love of Christ to your spouse, you have **real love** in your marriage...of a different but enduring type. Abide in the love of Christ, and you will be or become attractive to your spouse, and they may soon be catching feelings for you again.

M for Money Matters

"According to Crown Financial Ministries the number one factor in the breakup of most marriages is financial discord. 85% of marriages that fail do so because of financial problems. And this kind of financial turmoil is no less of a problem in many Christian marriages..." (Barry R. Leventhal, Ph.D., Crosswalk.com, REF 2c).

"Couples who reported disagreeing about finances once a week were 30 percent more likely to get divorced than couples who reported disagreeing about them once a month, according to a Utah State University study" (Renee Morad, Money Talks News, REF 2d).

"Money issues are also responsible for 22% of all divorces, making it the third leading cause, according to the Institute for Divorce Financial Analysis" (Jennifer Ryan Woods, Forbes, REF 2e).

I WILL ADMIT STRAIGHT OFF the bat that I feel unqualified to write about this very extensive topic. Firstly, I haven't always had the right attitude towards finances and financial planning. I am one of those unfortunate people who underestimated the importance of money in marriage. And secondly, I've still got a long way to go to get my act together. Like the saying goes, "*old habits die hard*" (REF 4i).

This issue of money must be raised from the moment someone is talking about marriage in a relationship. It shouldn't be postponed until later, because it might seem unromantic, or greedy, or even unholy. Let's face it, marriage is of the world... And money is of the world too. The two have relations - a practical relationship! When two people come together, it is not simply their bodies or their hearts that are united but their finances and assets too.

Five things that must be addressed early on is each person's:

1. Attitude to money. Are they greedy or stingy? Are they frugal or careless? Are they generous or charitable to a fault? Is it easy come easy go, or are they financially shrewd? Do you agree with, like, or disrespect the other person's attitude to money? Do you suspect that your partner might actually *love* money? Do you love money?

2. Spending habits. Do they live within their means? Do they shop to impress others? Do they have debt, and is the debt growing, or are they paying off their debts? Do they pay taxes and other fines they may owe or incur? Do they tend to buy assets or consumables or services? Are they penny wise, pound foolish? Are they rich in spirit, living by faith on credit cards and lacking in godly contentment? Does their spending make you feel safe or anxious?

3. Financial goals. Do they have any? Do they believe

in having goals of any kind? Are their goals realistic? Do their goals reveal flawed priorities? Maybe they are more career focused than family focused. Maybe they are more independently minded and not relationship conscious. Do you agree with and believe in their goals?

4. Strategy for financial independence and stability. Do they actually have a plan to achieve their goals? Is their plan realistic? Where do you factor in each other's plans? Does their lifestyle agree with their goals and strategic plan?

5. Capital. What do they have materially? Are they honest about their financial status? Are they in debt or indebted? Do they own assets, like a car or home or land or business etc? Are they too poor (too rich?) for you? Are they financially comfortable or needy?

The problem is, when we leave these discussions until after we have invested ourselves emotionally into each other, one or both partners may be bamboozled by 'love' to enter a marriage that is financially problematic or doomed. It is like driving under the influence. You really don't process the information properly. You take short cuts in your thinking. You assume too much, and your judgement is off. You make hasty decisions, and then you find yourself in a mess. But you still have to get over your hangover and clean up the mess before you can actually get back on track.

It is a fact that, for a majority of marriages, finance is a huge concern, even if it is not a problem. Finance is always going to be a concern, even if you marry a filthy rich man (or woman), with little or no care in the world. If they worked hard for that money, they will care about your attitude to money and spending habits. If you are not prudent with money, even if there is lots of it, there will be arguments and problems in your marriage because of your attitude or carelessness.

It is essential to have compatibility in this regard. The more agreement you have, the less conflict you will have over finances, and the greater your respect will be for the financial habits and decisions of your partner. However, the less agreement you have, the more arguments you will have about finances, and the lower your respect will be for each other.

"The Utah State University study found individuals who feel their spouse spends money foolishly reported lower levels of marital happiness and gauged their likelihood of divorce at 45 percent" (Renee Morad, Money Talks News, REF 2d).

An environment of disagreement and tension also breeds secrecy and distrust, which we have seen is the enemy of intimacy. So, besides the financial problems you are having, your incompatibility has already added a problematic barrier, which you must first break through to finally resolve your financial issues as a team. It is extremely important to be transparent, and to maintain transparency, by openly and frequently talking about your finances so that such barriers are not allowed to grow and hinder you from tackling your financial challenges together.

Having agreement and transparency doesn't mean that you will be successful financially. Especially if you are both financially foolish. You can both agree never to talk about your finances. You can both agree to spend yourselves to the ground. You can both agree never to invest or save, or plan for your retirement, or even do family planning. You can both agree to live on charity, loans, and social services. Yes, you may not argue, since you have agreement. But when you're both flat broke, the blame and the resentment will be all that will keep you company. But at least you are in it together.

So, apart from agreement and transparency, there is a need to be financially wise. Not greedy. Not worrying. Not striving. But practical, critical, diligent, responsible, and generous.

Yes, it is important to also be generous. Jesus taught that "*…it is more blessed to give than to receive*" (Acts 20:35). As Believers, we must recognise money for what it is - a tool. We don't work for money, as though having financial wealth is our reward. We work for God and use money to achieve the purposes God created us for, including being charitable towards the less fortunate.

We put money to work in industry and also in leisure. So, we must be good stewards of money, even as we enjoy the rewards of our diligence. Here is a saying worth remembering; "*Food for the stomach and the stomach for food, but God will destroy them both*" (1 Cor 6:13). When we rightly handle money, we will enjoy it, without glorifying it or serving it. But we must honour God and put our trust in Him as the One who is our great REWARD (Gen 15:1).

We must never forget that we own nothing of ourselves. All that we have belongs to God, and we will one day give account of how we used the resources He has given us. It is important that both partners have the same understanding of this role of money and God's sovereignty. If you disagree on this, you will most likely disagree on your attitudes towards money and your spending habits too, and you will find yourself in a turbulent marriage.

Here are five things you should be doing to ensure sound financial health in your marriage, if you haven't already begun to do so:

> 1. Talk about your finances, and be open and honest with each other about your attitudes and spending, goals and plans, and current financial circumstances;

> 2. Agree on a budgeting plan for your household going forward. There are many ideas out there. Choose one that will work for you (as a couple or family);

> 3. Start saving and investing. Think critically, and plan for

unforeseen events, children, retirement, and yes, holidays too;

4. Get out of debt! Start living within your means, cut down on unnecessary spending; **rethink, reduce, reuse, recycle**;

5. Get financial counsel and help. Yes, it is that important. Finance may not be your strongest point; you may not have much interest in it, but you must address it before it endangers your marriage.

Money matters in marriage. Don't deny it. Don't ignore it. Don't run from it. Don't lie about it. Deal with it. Honestly. Together. In submission to God.

N for Nobody's Perfect; Negotiate and Never Give Up

JESUS SAID, "*THE TRUTH will set you free*" (John 8:33), and of course, He was right. He meant Himself! He is the Truth that sets us free (John 14:6). But knowledge of AND acceptance of *any* truth always brings freedom.

There is a truth that ought to bring many captives of difficult marriages freedom today, and that is the truth that NO ONE IS PERFECT. No, not them, not their spouse, and not any imaginary knight in shining armour or princess that they hope will save them from their miserable marriage.

Living with imperfect people is not only a fact of life...it is also a JOY of life! The sooner you embrace this truth, the sooner you will set yourself and your spouse free from the bondage of unrealistic expectations and start to truly KNOW and appreciate each other as you ought to. **Marriage is a beautiful mess of two imperfect people, learning to appreciate and love each other unconditionally.** As hard as it may be, you gotta love it, and when you persevere in it, it brings forth a beautiful fruit in your spirit and in your union.

Maybe you already know that no one is perfect and can admit that you are not perfect. Maybe you do not expect perfection from your spouse, but yet they fall short of your minimal standards, and you wonder...even if there's no one perfect, surely, they can do better! You're probably right. But, as we saw when we dealt with expectations in marriage, you could be wrong too.

After you have accepted that no one is perfect, the next thing to accept is that no two people are the same. You are both different, and difference is okay. Difference is good. Difference is beautiful! Accept it, and find a way to NEGOTIATE your differences, and find common ground for your continued fellowship.

Stop trying to see every disagreement as right versus wrong. If you do, you're always going to be wrong because the only one that was ever right was Christ. Right is where you are both going from being at different levels of wrong, and you won't get there by yourself. You need your teammate, and you both need to be dropping some of your ideas and opinions and drawing closer to right...to Wisdom. This journey requires lots of understanding, lots of humility, and lots of grace.

You may find that, even after you have exercised grace and humility to your spouse and tried to be understanding of your differences and their flaws and shortcomings, you are still faced with someone who NEEDS to change. They may be abusive. They may be uncompromising, such that you are the only one bending to them... They may be blatantly walking in sin and error.

Sure no one is perfect, but we shouldn't excuse people who are abusive, who make no efforts to grow or change or walk in love. What then? Do we walk away from our marriage, when we have pledged to love and honour our spouse until death separates us? Do we give up?

NO! We should not. Because that is not what LOVE would do. Remember, love never fails... (1 Cor 13:8). Love covers a multitude of sins (1 Pet 4:8). We must NEVER give up (Gal 6:9)! We must abide in love - in Christ - that the power of God may be unleashed in our marriage (John 15:1-5).

Be faithful in prayer. Be long-suffering in trials. Be kind with offences. Be ever hopeful and ever believing...in God. Do not lay your hope in Man, but in God who is at work in your marriage to the glory of His own name.

This is how we show our faith. Faith is not required when things are easy, when the odds are in our favour. Faith is required when the road is hard and bleak and the obstacles seem insurmountable. It may be impossible for men...but ALL THINGS ARE POSSIBLE FOR HIM WHO BELIEVES (Mark 9:23).

The world will tell you it is hopeless. That your spouse will never change. They will quote statistics. They will turn your gaze to yourself...talking about what you deserve.

You deserve the punishment Christ paid for your salvation on the Cross. He gave you life, so the life you now live, you ought to live for Him who died for you (Gal 2:20).

In everything, think of your spouse (Phil 2:3). Think of the duty of love that you owe them, which is unconditional. Think of how God is about to turn the situation around, and how your faithfulness is key to the testimony of your trial.

Remember that whatever evil they may do, they "*know not what they do*" (Luke 23:34). Jesus wasn't lying. Those who are taken by the enemy to do evil are blind and need deliverance. And however evil they may seem, no one is beyond redemption. Allow yourself to be used by God, so that you may even save your spouse through your perseverance in love. Who knows if that was not the reason for your union in marriage (1 Cor 7:16)?

However, I surely hope that you are not going through the worse end of marriage. If you're suffering, seek help and counselling from Christian Marriage Counsellors, and let them pray for you and your spouse. Regarding issues of domestic violence, it will be needful to separate and protect yourself and any affected children from harm. I have more to say on the issue of domestic violence and divorce, but for now, it is good to remember two things:

1. "*If anyone does not provide for his own, and especially his own household, he has denied the faith and is worse than an unbeliever*" (1 Tim 5:8). If such is said for those who neglect their family, what can be said for those who violently abuse them?

2. "*But if the unbeliever leaves, let him go. The believing brother or sister is not bound in such cases. God has called you to live in peace*" (1 Cor 7:15). An abuser is an unbeliever, no matter their profession by mouth. If you can be free, be free of them, for "...*you were bought at a price; do not become slaves of men*" (1 Cor 7:23).

Love an abuser as you would love your enemy, without paying evil for evil (Rom 12:17-21). You wouldn't fellowship with your enemy, so you need not be intimate with an abuser. But free them with forgiveness from your heart, and continually pray for their deliverance, believing by faith that God is able to restore them... And walk in the LIBERTY that Christ has called you to walk (Gal 5:1).

O for Offspring

"The only things you can count on are chaos and each other and somehow that's okay because it's a perfect kind of beautiful chaos as you see each other more clearly and know you're right where you wanna be, lack of sleep, spit up, noise and all" (Paula Rollo, REF 4j).

O FFSPRING, ALSO KNOWN AS children, are one of the fruits of a blessed marriage. The Bible says children are a gift from God and regards them as the fruit of the womb (Psa 127:3). It is right to desire to have children, but it is more important to be mature enough to look after them and raise them up with the love and admonition of God (Prov 22:6, Eph 6:4).

Not every marriage is blessed with children or the fruit of the womb. This can cause a problem for the couple, depending on their desire for children and their expectations from marriage. If they married in order to have a family and raise children, then not being able to conceive can feel like a failure. However, as we saw in B for Blessed to Bless, children are not the confirmation that your marriage is blessed. A marriage without children is still blessed by God and will bear fruit if rightly handled.

Like the idea of getting married, the idea of having children needs to be forsaken and left at the feet of Jesus when one becomes a Believer. It can be very hard for us to lay down these desires, which are natural and good, but just as we must lay down our lives to follow Jesus, these also must be laid down (Luke 14:26). **If we refuse to lay them down, we will not receive them as the *gifts* that they are if and when God decides to bless us with them.** We will covet, we will be discontent, we will scheme, and we will sin in our desire to have them. Thus, we will forfeit the joy that comes from being submitted to God in every aspect of our lives.

If we do end up getting married or having children, by our own wilfulness and means, it is also likely that, since we have not learned to follow and submit to God, we will not value the gifts of marriage and childbearing. We will likely misuse these gifts or not be mature enough to show our spouse and children the love of God. But someone who has forsaken the idea of getting married, and God grants them this gift in His mercy, will be more appreciative and will be more able to hear and follow God in their marriage and in their new role as a parent too.

Just as marriage, being a gift, comes with its challenges, children also come with their challenges. Too many people fantasise about having children without realising how great a responsibility they are and the need for them to be ready to raise them right. The saying goes that *"marriage is the only school where you get the certificate before you start…"* (REF 4k). Likewise, with parenthood. In fact, there is no certification, nor mandatory parent counselling, nothing to prepare you for the many ways your life will change once you hear the word 'pregnant.' What there is is a lot of pressure from every angle (your family, friends, community, the Media, and even the

Church) to have a baby, through false expectations laid on newlyweds.

Yes, we have prenatal classes, doctor's visits, and lots and lots of information online now about parenthood and what to expect. We also have, if we are lucky, experienced and wise parents and elders to guide us. These don't help you with the financial implications, they don't help you with the practical implications, or the emotional, sexual, physical changes your body (and marriage) will go through. They may ease your anxieties and help you feel more in control, but there's nothing like real experience to teach you and shape you into the parent you ought to be.

Having children will change you as a person and change your relationship as a couple FOREVER! Hopefully, your children will outlive you. Once you become a parent, you will always be a parent, so the cost implications are life-long. You can't shirk your responsibility onto someone else. When thinking and planning for a baby, you have to realise the weight of what you are undergoing, and be sober about the LIFE you are bringing into the world and your responsibility as its GUARDIAN.

I make no claim to being an expert at raising children. At the time I penned this chapter, I only had the experience of parenting one and the experience of the wonder that is pregnancy and childbirth. I also know, from real experience, the changes that I went (and I am still going) through joggling marriage and motherhood, as well as work and ministry. Even though our experiences will be different, there are many similarities in our stories, and we can all learn from other people's experiences while recognising that our own story may be very different.

With all this said, here are five points I hope you will take away from this chapter:

1. FORSAKE IT – There are many people living with a hole in their heart because they have not been able to conceive, or maybe, they haven't had as many children as they wanted…or maybe they want a girl and only have boys, or they want a boy and only have girls. You can fulfil your purpose without childbearing or raising children. If you genuinely want to raise (one or more) children, then consider adoption. Who ever said that you can only raise your own children? There are many children living without the love and protection of a parent. Maybe there's a place in your home and heart for one of them.

2. BE FAITHFUL WITH THE LITTLE THINGS

– Jesus said that no one will entrust true riches to someone who has been faithless with little, but if we are faithful with the little things, God will entrust us with much (Luke 16:10-12). There are some people who are ready to throw away their marriage because they don't have a child. That is a classic example of someone who cannot be trusted with true riches… They haven't even been faithful with what God has already bestowed on them. They haven't appreciated their gift but have despised it while coveting greater blessing. Rather, use your marriage as an opportunity to grow in love and to mature in every way…and if God decides to bless your home with a child, you will be ready to handle that *added* blessing.

3. BE SOBER

– Children are not accessories or assets that you can get with your buying power. Every human life is valuable and priceless and must be regarded with all sobriety. They are not to add to your status, nor your own value, but are a responsibility for which you must give account to God on how you raised them. Do not seek to have children because everyone expects you to, everyone is doing it, you are getting old, you are bored, or any other self-centred reason. When thinking or planning to have children, consider their soul…consider the environment you are bringing them into, consider how God will use you in raising up a child of purpose, who will make a positive impact in the world, not merely make you smile for a while and get people off your back. This is a decision you should make as a couple, listening to each other and appreciating each person's desire and perspective. If you are not united, it is better to forsake it than to bring a child into disunity.

4. BE RESPONSIBLE – We have seen that marriage is a gift and a responsibility and considered all the ways we must grow in love to succeed in this vocation. Raising children requires as much dedication, if not more. Just as money matters in marriage, money matters in raising children. Sure, you don't have to be rich to have children, just as you don't have to be rich to get married, but you've got to be financially conscious and responsible, and you've got to plan for EACH of your children. You can think of it this way; do unto others as you would have them do to you. What you would have wanted your parents to do for you, you should do for your child, and even more, since our world is a different place from when you were a child.

5. ENJOY IT! – It is a gift! And a joyous one at that! There's a reason many desire to have children. No matter the sacrifices, no matter the pains, no matter the challenges they bring, raising them is part of the joy of living. The circle of life, as some might say. If we have been blessed to have children, we shouldn't forget to enjoy the process of transformation such a blessing brings to our lives as we grow from being new parents to mature and responsible guardians, who are training the leaders of tomorrow. We must also make sure that we allow our children to enjoy being children. We shouldn't burden them with our burdens, rather we should give them a chance to enjoy the phase of life that is childhood.

In all of this, you have to remember that your marriage comes first. In most cases, you would have pledged your love and commitment to your spouse before your child was even conceived. Your marriage was the bearer of the child, and it would be a travesty if the child becomes the destruction of your marriage. By giving your marriage its rightful place of honour, you are CAPABLE of giving your child the love, care, and protection it needs to grow into a mature and responsible adult, who has been groomed for success. Never put the cart before the horse.

Do not lose sight of your spouse nor neglect your responsibilities to them because of the arrival of a child. Even as the child is most demanding, you have to make EXTRA effort to pay attention to the needs of your spouse and to keep working as a team. Don't start working against each other or working on your own and seeing your spouse as the intruder or your enemy. You need each other to succeed at parenthood, marriage, and life! Remember that your fortunes are tied forever.

Soon your children will grow up and move away from home and become independent of you. They will likely have their own marriages and families. Remember that their experience in your home is what will serve as a pattern for what they will aspire to in their own homes. They will imitate you, whether consciously or not, so you need to show them, by example, the esteem they must show to their spouses and the wisdom of preserving the marital bond even above the maternal or paternal bonds. It will be a source of inspiration to them to see your marriage and love still going strong, long after they have left your abode.

P for Passion, Purpose, and Prosperity

P**ASSION. WHAT WOULD YOU** be without it? Dead, I suppose. Passion is our drive. We must be passionate about something enough to hope for its fulfilment and keep on living.

Passion is not synonymous with love but with strong emotion. A vocation such as marriage calls for passion. The person we have pledged to share our lives with needs to know that we feel passionately for them and that we are passionate about our commitment enough to weather any storms that may lie ahead.

Aside from having passion for your spouse, you will and should have passion for other things in life. Though it may be the fantasy of many, no one can truly handle being the sole passion of another person. They will feel drained. Used. Caged. Frustrated. Such intense passion (aka obsession) may even dampen whatever passion they have for you. It is needful to have other things in life that stir you up, make you happy, and bring out the best of your potential. This also makes you an all-round attractive person. So, if you are looking for a mate, pursue your passions.

You may not know your passions early, but when you meet the one you want to spend the rest of your life with, you will KNOW them by how they **illuminate** your other passions in life. They will *confirm* your passions, even if they do not share your passions completely. They will *fuel* your passion, inspire you to dream and achieve. One thing they will not do is stand in the way of you and your passion. This is one way you can tell who is meant for you.

And just as they kindle and support your passion, you will do the same for them. You will connect on this level, and like 'yin and yang,' if I may use that, you will FIT. If you are Christian, one of your mutual passions, which will bind you ever closer, will be your passion for Christ. Because you are both passionate for Christ, one will not be pulling the other down or away from God, but both will encourage and inspire each other to a deeper fellowship with God and good works towards all men. And as you meet this need to grow deeper into God, your relationship will be filled with joy and passion.

PURPOSE. When you key into your passion, you will identify your purpose in life. I believe that God has given us each passions so that we may have a purposeful existence. And some of us (not all) will find a partner in a spouse, to assist us in achieving our purpose. **Marriage, itself, is not the purpose of our existence. If we act like it is, we will be miserable, even in marriage.**

Woman was given to man, first for a COMPANION (aka Friend) and then a HELPER (aka Partner), that together, they may have dominion over their world. The union of marriage has purpose. Every individual has a purpose. It therefore connects that your individual purposes will merge without conflict to support a united purpose in marriage. If, however, you observe that your passions do not relate, and your purposes seem deviated, it would be foolish to assume that you have any business together in marriage.

Many go their whole lives never knowing who they are, let alone their purpose. They may have many passions; some may even be conflicting. Some people may feel like they have no passion at all. You may be one of those people. Don't worry about it. Simply do what you love and what you do well. This will ignite your passion and help you to discover your purpose. Even people who followed what they believed was their purpose early in life may have learnt more about themselves and discovered a new and different purpose along the way. It comes with maturity. It also comes with knowing God.

The main point I would like to make here is that if you know God...you will *know* your spouse if and when you meet such a person. You won't be confused about your purpose. You won't be immature about your passions. And you will easily identify them by how you connect on both passion and purpose. They will also easily identify you because, if you are walking with God, your mate will most certainly also be found in Him (2 Cor 6:14). So, if you want to know your mate, get to know God...

PROSPERITY. Prosperity is the inevitable end when you walk in passion and purpose. The Bible says, "*he who finds a wife finds a good thing and obtains favor from the LORD*" (Prov 18:22).

To clarify, prosperity is not the goal. It is the FRUIT! You should never go in search of prosperity, otherwise, you will be blinded by the deceitfulness of riches. You will be as one chasing a butterfly. You also do not marry so that you will find favour. That's not what the verse says. It says that

WHEN you have found your wife (who connects with your passion and purpose), you will receive God's favour in your marriage.

Prosperity may not spring up suddenly in your marriage. Don't assume that if you are married and you are not yet prosperous, that it means you have not received favour from God... Don't ever fall for the trick that you must have married the wrong person, which is why you are not experiencing favour, so you need to divorce and marry the right person to be blessed. God is merciful, and He honours our marriages, as we have seen in B for Blessed to Bless. Even if we made a mistake, God will use our marriage to teach us and bring out our godly nature if we are willing to submit.

The difference is, if we had obeyed God and followed His guidance *before* marriage, we would not find ourselves in a marriage where we are constantly striving. Both partners would have been at a place of maturity, where both are following God, and as such, are already walking in His love and grace. They will begin to enjoy the favour of the Lord on their union from the beginning, and the natural challenges that come with life will be easily overcome because they are a STRONG and ORDAINED unit, and they put their trust in God.

Once you are married, however, your partner is Mr Right or Mrs Right. If your passions and purposes are conflicting, it is time for you to do some FORSAKING. In your marriage vows, you would have promised to FORSAKE ALL OTHERS for the sake of your union. You will need to rediscover your passions, and work together on a new and UNITED purpose. The greatest and most promising purpose any couple can have is to glorify God with their marriage. If that is your purpose, you will most certainly succeed because you are lined up with God, going where He is going, and He is going to help you.

Forsake all you ever thought your life would be and discover all that your life COULD be if you will make the effort to get to know God and know your partner more intimately. This can be a great adventure, depending on your attitude. It will be hard at first to forsake these dreams, which may have kept you hopeful all these years. But you are not forsaking them for nothing; you are forsaking them for Christ - the Pearl of great price (Matt 13:45-46). You are forsaking them to learn LOVE and to bear the most blessed fruit in your marriage, which is a union that looks like Christ and the Church. And on this mission, you will certainly find new passion, purpose, and prosperity in life.

Q for Quality over Quantity

WE LIVE IN A SOCIETY THAT seems to value quantity over quality, even though we like to chant "quality over quantity." Our actions show that we do not truly believe this. We want more, it doesn't so much matter that the things we are gathering are insignificant, only that we have LOTS of it! Isn't that stupid?

Somehow, we reckon that if we had enough QUANTITY it would inevitably add up to QUALITY of life... But this is a lie from the pit of hell! It is a lie from the Thief and Father of Lies, who comes to rob us of our valuable time, precious worth, and irreplaceable joy (John 10:10)! This is the spirit of Greed that has overtaken the world (1 Tim 6:9-10).

There is a reason the perpetual rat race is called such; because it is an unending and purposeless pursuit of something unattainable - ENOUGH. There is no such thing as enough *quantitatively* speaking. And besides, enough never made anyone happy because there is still more. If we think and evaluate in terms of quantity, we will never be satisfied with what we have, even if we were the richest person in the world.

A human is not a physical container that can be filled with stuff. Stuff can never make us happy. Stuff is good only for the *body*. But we are made of so much more than flesh...

We desire and need something more intangible, to fill us...our minds and hearts and spirits. We should rather think in terms of quality, seeking what is good and worthwhile. With a qualitative mindset, we can have enough...also known as CONTENTMENT. With the spirit of Contentment, we can appreciate life, even if we are poor materially (Phil 4:12, 1 Tim 6:8). We can be satisfied and happy.

The Bible has some more things to say about this:

"Of course, godliness with contentment is great gain" (1 Tim 6:6).

"Better is a dry morsel and quietness with it than a house full of feasting with strife" (Prov 17:1).

"Better is the poor who walks in his integrity than he who is crooked though he be rich" (Prov 28:6).

There is a wisdom that goes, "less is more," but we often grumble at the less rather than appreciating all the ways it blesses us. It is in the darkness that we can appreciate the stars. It is in facing trials that we can grow in character. It is in solitude that we can know and appreciate our individuality and spirituality. Sometimes, it takes poverty for us to realise the many free gifts of God abounding in nature.

The Notorious B.I.G is known for saying, "*more money, more problems*" (REF 5c), and there appears to be some sense to that, though Steve Siebold would disagree (REF 2f). Well, I think money is like a baby; you've got to spend money on it to help it grow and keep it safe. You look after your money in your youth, so that it will look after you in your old age... *Did someone say insurance?* The more of it you have, the more diligent and accountable you must be. **Unfortunately for some, money is the only 'baby' they will have or treasure. Everything is forsaken to keep it, and over the years, the true cost of their misplaced priorities becomes more apparent.**

If we even consider our society that is so rich, so more 'advanced,' so more knowledgeable, we can see that we have traded wisdom for knowledge, relationships for possessions, and health for wealth... The former seemed too abstract to quantify, so we went for what we could COUNT! Too many people are "penny wise, pound foolish" in this regard or "quantity wise, quality foolish." Incredibly, you can have a thousand degrees and still be stupid!

This phenomenal stupidity is a root cause of why marriages are failing; because we value possessions over relationships. We do not know how to LIVE like humans anymore, nor how to treat others like humans who need emotional, spiritual, and physical connections. Rather, we treat ourselves and others as OBJECTS to be possessed. Everything and everyone is now for sale and, as such, exchangeable, replaceable, and dispensable.

We now need others to add value to us in terms of quantity and monetary figures. Even motherhood has a price, and the housewife now needs to value her contribution to the household in dollars! Why do we need others to tell us our worth? We need to know our worth without seeking validation from others.

If we do not have the right mindset, then we are truly poor, and we will have nothing to bring into a relationship, not to talk of marriage. You can only give what you have...and those who are deficient need constantly to be replenished. Their poverty of mind will deplete whatever their spouse brings to the table, as they nag and quarrel, strive and accuse, lusting continually, but never finding fulfilment for their needs (Jam 4:1-3). They will spend their time constantly seeking to acquire more things, rather than enjoying the priceless gifts they didn't earn nor buy; their spouse and children, their health, and the natural world.

But with the right mindset, you are indeed rich in all things. You will be rich in wisdom, joy, holiness, and contentment. You will be able to appreciate the simple things in life. You will be grateful for the big and small efforts your spouse makes to spend time with you. You will maximise every opportunity to bring out quality in your relationships, and you will not depend on quantity of time nor quantity of stuff to make you happy.

Before you can appreciate and prioritise quality in your marriage, you have to first develop your qualitative reasoning about life. You have to change your mindset, change your values, change your assessment of worth. You need a renewal of your mind, drawing your identity and value from what God says about you, knowing how greatly He valued you, enough to lay down His life for you...

When you are of a right mind, the difference can be as pronounced as appreciating a 30 minutes family home-cooked meal at the table over a two-hour meal at a restaurant. Appreciating ten minutes of laughing and dancing in your living room over three hours at the cinema. Or even appreciating how your busted TV has created more time for family games and conversations...

This is not to say dinner outings, trips to the cinema, or casual watching of TV at home are bad things. But perspective makes all the difference. The question is really WHAT do you value more? What do you want out of life?

Is it the amount of time spent or the quality of time spent? Is it the places you go to or who you go there with? Is it what you do together or how you feel when you do those things together? If you know what you REALLY want, you will be more purposeful about getting it and will appreciate the ways you are already blessed, rather than live in discontent over what you may not have.

R for Respect is Reciprocal

"Nevertheless, let everyone of you in particular so love his wife even as himself; and the wife see that she reverence her husband" (Ephesians 5:33).

DO YOU KNOW WHAT THE VERSE above is saying? Do you know what it is *not* saying? Many use this and other verses to imply that a wife owes her husband respect, reverence, and submission while she shouldn't expect such from him. Except, of course, his love.

However, have you ever seen someone love without submission? Even Jesus submitted Himself to His followers. He washed their feet (John 13:4-5). He told them He came to serve and not to be served (Matt 20:28). He died for them! And Paul tells us that husbands should love their wives in a like manner (Eph 5:25).

Okay, so we have to admit that for one to love another, they must submit to the other. If we consider the preceding verse before this section on marriage, *"...submitting yourselves one to another in the fear of God"* (Eph 5:21), we can see that we are all called to loving submission. Obviously, by Paul telling the husbands to love their wives as themselves, he wasn't suggesting that the wives shouldn't love their husbands as they do themselves, so why should we conclude that respect in marriage is a one-way street?

What Paul was doing was laying EMPHASIS, based on the tendencies of both sexes and the unique needs of the sexes. Women are naturally more emotional and in need of some pampering. Men often need to be reminded to be sensitive, so it was right for Paul to admonish them to love their wives as themselves. They may, otherwise, take their wife's emotional needs for granted. We have already talked about the importance of romance and the husband's duty to keep this alive in marriage.

Likewise, men have a great need for respect and honour, and as the leaders in marriage, they need to be held in *special* honour. Wives that appreciate their equal standing in Christ and in life may not fully realise their need to always show respect and reverence to their husband, who is ultimately the leader. So, Paul was right to lay emphasis on this duty of married women.

So, while wives must love their husbands, as they do themselves, they must not forget to hold them in honour and reverence too. And while husbands must respect their wives as equals and bearers of the Spirit of God, they must not forget to give them due love and affection too. *Simples!*

Respect, like love, must be reciprocal! We cannot demand respect when we don't give respect. Do you know that even GOD respects humans...? As poor, depraved, and inconsequential as we are, He respects us. Wasn't it God who made clothes for Adam and Eve when they found out that they were naked in the Garden of Eden? He respected their shame, and He covered them up. God respects us so much that He gave us free will. So, who is the 'king' that will reign in his house and deny his own wife respect...because of what?

Even though respect is commanded, it is also a right of *every* human being. There is no special status you must gain before you receive respect. As long as you are human, respect is your basic right.

However, it is easier to respect someone who behaves in a respectable and respectful way, just as it is easier to love someone who is loving and loveable. We can all do more to earn respect from our spouse, even if it is also our right, and even if they are commanded to show it. It shouldn't be hard for them to love us, and we shouldn't make it hard for them to respect us either.

Now, it would seem that because of this emphasis laid on wives to respect their husbands, that husbands should show respect in *response* to the respect their wives show them... WRONG! We really shouldn't be doing this tit for tat. We really should come 100%, ready to even outdo our spouse in love and respect. But if there is someone to set the pace...someone to set the standard...someone to lead the way, it would be - you guessed it - the HUSBAND! He is after all the leader.

Just as Christ didn't wait for us to show Him love before He bestowed us with His amazing love and grace... Just as Christ submitted Himself to the Cross, even before we proved our worth, so likewise, husbands must *go first*... They must lead by example. They must model respect, submission, and love so that their wives will IMITATE their humility, just as followers of Jesus imitate His humility. And like Jesus said, whoever seeks to be the greatest or the master, they must be the least and the servant (Matt 20:26-27).

A Christian man, a follower of Jesus Christ, cannot miss this message. This is a truth that they should know if they have the Lord's Spirit. So, any man using Scripture to put his wife in her place doesn't know God. But a man who knows God and is walking with God will be humble, loving, submissive, and WORTHY of all respect. His wife will not need to be told to respect him... In fact, she will be in AWE of him and will sing his praises everywhere.

So, if you are constantly fighting with your wife for respect and authority in your house, consider the example you have given for humble, loving submission. Check yourself, follow Jesus, and she *will* follow you.

Now that that is cleared up... Ladies, respect your husbands! In case you are struggling to understand the emphasis laid on you, here are FIVE reasons you ought to respect him:

1. He is a human being too. Must I say more? The respect you give to others is the respect you demand for yourself. Do not hold back... Do unto others, as you would have them do to you (Luke 6:31).

2. He is a Servant of God. If indeed he is a Christian, he is a Man of God and worthy of special honour for this alone. You owe all your Christian brothers and sisters special honour for being in the Family of God, and your husband is not exempt at all (Gal 6:10).

3. He is the man you love. Well, I am guessing you *love* him because you pledged your life to him, to be his wife. I'm also guessing there was something uniquely fabulous about him that got him the privilege of your companionship for the rest of his life... And the fact that he was *smart* enough to pick you as his life partner, *girl*...you gotta respect him!

4. He is the head of your home. If you could stack respect, the kind of respect you should have for your husband now should be level 3! Now, not only is he a human being, child of God, and the love of your life, he also happens to be given the special duty of heading your home - by God! That's a whole lot of responsibility and, as such, it deserves its own respect. So, we're at level 4. Remember the Scripture, "*give honour to whom honour is due*" (Rom 13:7). Honouring your husband as the head of your home is your obedience to Christ. It is your Christianity.

5. He is the father of your children. As if you need more reason to respect your husband... As the father of your children, even if he is not the biological father of your children, the fact that he is raising your children, he is worthy of respect. Respect him because his role needs and demands it, but also because your children are watching you and learning from you about what is good and right and loving. Respect him for the ways he provides for you and your family, and protects and cares for you all, fulfilling his duty of love.

I think we all know what respect looks like. Sometimes, though, the word can be scary, depending on the context in which it is used and who is wielding it. Respect can be as simple as giving due regard to another human being, or showing deep admiration to someone for their achievements and exercise of duty, or even as reverence and awe for their power and authority...like the respect we have for God. Give all men and women their due respect, not the reverence due only to God.

Respect and submission have been abused in many homes and cultures. I hope to liberate my Christian sisters with the truth about what godly respect and submission requires. This is what respect for your husband looks like:

1. Allowing them to take the lead. Learn to follow their lead, even if you think you know better. This is what it means to be humble and submissive. If you *never* think you know better and can do it better, it would be no trouble at all to *always* follow your husband's lead. So being humble and submissive is a recognition of the fact that you are not a stupid dummy, but you are simply forsaking your opinion or way for the sake of your unity.

2. Showing admiration and appreciation of them. We all know women love to be showered with admiration and praise. Sometimes, we forget that men do too. They want to be recognised for their strengths and the effort they put in loving you and caring for you. Respect them by acknowledging the big or small things they do, saying "thank you" often, praising them in private and in public. Knowing that you admire and appreciate them is a validation that they are doing okay (or even great) as husbands.

3. Giving them veto power. As the head of your home, they should have the last say. Why? Because they will give account to God as the leader, just as the President of any country will give account to God for the people he presided over and the decisions he allowed or denied. So, you respect your husband by running things by him, by obeying him when he says not to do certain things or he says to do certain things. If you are having a disagreement, be the one to rescind or forsake your opinion, trusting that they are following God too. Always give their opinion due regard, and make sure that you don't do anything in DISAGREEMENT with them. If they say "no," appeal to God, and if they are following God, God will counsel them on the way to go.

4. Serve them in honour. Jesus commanded his followers not to rule like the kings of the world but to be servants (Matt 20:25-28). Your *Christian* husband *will not* lord his position over you. But as he humbles himself before you and God, God will use YOU to exalt him by serving him... So, even if he doesn't particularly ask for it, or demand certain privileges, give them to him without him having to ask. Treat him like he is a *king* because he is actually a king, just a humble one. Speak with him kindly. Serve his meals with extra care and attention. Wait on him... Pamper him... If you do these things, he will not take it as reason to lord himself over you, rather, it will fuel his love, desire, and respect for you as a woman of honour.

5. Showing them unconditional positive regard. Okay, we know that not all men will be easy to respect, even if they are Christian. There are many different personalities out there. And not all men are good husbands or good leaders or good fathers. They may not be good providers. They may not be good lovers. They may not even be good listeners. But respect them by *always* showing them acceptance, support, and grace.

Recognise their strengths and weaknesses, and build on their strengths, while granting grace on their weaknesses. You can use their point of weakness to identify where you can take more responsibility and make up for their lack. You are after all their 'helper.' So, assist them in their responsibility over your family. Never talk down to them, never talk badly about them, and never give up on them.

You are the one God has chosen to use to build them up into the LEGEND they are going to be. You can't tear them down because you don't see the vision... In your long-suffering, call on God, and He will show you how He intends to use you to bless your husband and, by extension, your family, and He will grant you more grace to persevere.

So, I hope the message is clear here that respect is a two-way street, and women are not exempt from receiving respect from their husbands. In fact, *the husband ought to take the lead in showing humility and respect.* However, a wife is burdened to show greater honour to her husband as the head of her home, just as the President is esteemed above all other men.

Showing respect for someone else should never mean disrespect for yourself. Being a humble and submissive wife doesn't mean you have become the house slave... **But, just as Christ submitted Himself freely and beautifully, without losing any of His regality, you can give love and respect to your spouse without losing sight of who you are in Christ.**

S for Sex and Sexuality (1)

IT'S THE SUBJECT WE CAN'T AVOID. SEX! It's the most talked about subject, yet it is the most embarrassing and most misunderstood. A lot of the embarrassment and misunderstanding is to do with those who feel they are in power or control, communicating false messages to those who feel, or are made to feel, powerless about this thing called sex. And for lack of knowledge and understanding, the people perish indeed.

Marriages perish for lack of knowledge, understanding, and wisdom concerning sex. For most of their lives, people are told to shy away from anything sexual and given the impression that sex is a bad thing. If and when they talk about it, they do it secretly...because it is only 'bad people' who talk about sex openly, or so they are told. This means that people are not prepared to deal with sex in their marriage in a healthy way...

There has been some good reason for the scandal and fear that surrounds sex. Sex has been abused for almost as long as it has been practiced. People have misunderstood sex and made it a selfish venture when it was always supposed to be the expression of true love (unselfish) and the act of bonding between a man and his wife. It has been made into a commodity, a service that can be traded, a bargaining tool, and a weapon! And now, people don't really know what it is and how to appreciate it.

It's a bit like the discovery of fire. Fire has many uses, but it has been feared for as long as it has been known. Those who use it do so reverently, respectfully, knowing that the abuse of it would lead to fatal and catastrophic disasters. But still, man has explored how to control fire and manipulate it for the good of society. In regards to fire, men have been wise. But in regards to sex, not so much.

There are laws to everything in nature. We may know the laws, or we may not, but if we break them, we will suffer the consequences. Some laws are discovered by trial and error and passed on through education. And some laws are hidden until revealed by the Law Giver and passed on in commandments. The laws are for the benefit and safety of all people, not to put burdens on them. If we understand the purpose of the laws, and we understand that they *serve* us, we will honour them and not break nor violate them.

One of the laws of sex, which I would consider the FIRST, is that it is to be enjoyed *between* the sexes; that is two people of the opposite sex coming together to become one. Sex is not a gender issue, even though sex *informs* gender discourses. Sex is primarily a biological identity, while gender is a social construction, a produce of culture. Sex is factual. You are either male or female (with exception to those rare incidences of hermaphrodites, which is an abnormality).

Sexual activity is always and only supposed to be between a

person of the male sex and another of the female sex. Homosexuality and Lesbianism are contrary to *human* nature and sexuality (never mind what animals do). It doesn't take God to know this. Even science tells us that. Sexual intercourse between two people of the same sex cannot be qualified as legitimate sex, but it is a perversion, a rebellion, and an abomination. For me to say this blatantly is not to be homophobic nor hateful, but to be *truthful* and *loving*.

Sex serves the biological purpose of procreation and sustenance of the human race. It is primarily biological. But it is also a social, emotional, and physically enjoyable activity between two people of the opposite sex. However, there is another law that guides us in how sex should be practiced and who should engage in it. It is a spiritual law of love and wisdom.

Sex is meant to be practiced within the confines and safety of a marriage (a committed relationship and covenant between two people of the opposite sex). This is **wise** because, when practised this way, the rewards of sex are optimal for those engaged in it, their offspring, and the society at large. It is also **loving** because, in marriage, sex is a *service* to each other and not a selfish venture. It is the giving of yourself to another, wholly, being submitted and vulnerable to each other. And it enriches the relationship and continually binds the couple together.

Sexual intercourse is more than a biological activity, more than a physical activity, and even more than an emotional activity. There is also a spiritual element to sex, which binds those who engage in it beyond the physical union of their bodies. Such bonds are usually referred to as 'soul ties' and used to explain why people may feel drawn or bound to their first sexual partner or past sexual partners. It can also explain why those with multiple previous sexual partners often find it harder to settle and bind with their spouse in marriage.

Sexual immorality is an abuse of sex, which defies these

laws meant for their legitimate enjoyment. It is selfish, wicked, and offers no benefit to society. The Bible tells us to flee from sexual immorality and attests to the abomination of being joined to someone illegitimately, with the chastisements: "*...every sin that a man doeth is without the body; but he that committeth fornication sinneth against his own body. What? know ye not that your body is the temple of the Holy Ghost which is in you, which ye have of God, and ye are not your own?*" (1 Cor 6:18-19); and "*...what fellowship hath righteousness with unrighteousness? and what communion hath light with darkness? And what concord hath Christ with Belial? or what part hath he that believeth with an infidel?*" (2 Cor 6:14-15).

I won't dwell longer on sexual immorality, but it is important to address it in any discussion on sex. It is also needful to point out that marriage was made for man, not man for marriage. **And sex is as to marriage, as the fire is to the fire place. Within marriage, the practice of sex is safe, enjoyable, and beneficial to society, but apart from marriage, it is a scourge.** For "*Marriage is honourable in all, and the bed undefiled: but whoremongers and adulterers God will judge*" (Heb 13:4). It is plain to see that in the absence of sexual immorality, there would be no sexually transmitted diseases, but with the rampant practice of sexual immorality, even marriage becomes unsafe...

So, the rest of the discussion on the enjoyment of sex implies that it is practiced within marriage (between a man and a woman, in keeping with the first law of sex). The age of maturity to engage in sex or to give consent to sex differs across states and cultures, and there's no room for such a discourse here. We can also safely assume that those who will be engaged in marriage would have entered into the marriage knowledgeably, willingly, and lovingly, and are physically mature enough to enjoy sex.

In case it has been unclear, you need to know that GOD MADE SEX, so sex is good! It is meant to be enjoyed as well as rightly used. But like every good gift and every appealing pleasure, sex will always be susceptible to abuse by ungodly, deviant, and immature people. While sex is meant for marriage, marriage is greater than sex. A marriage should never be built on sex, but sex should be enjoyed within marriage, for that is the only avenue for it to be legitimately explored to the glory of God and the good of society. For more on this, read my blog post; HOW IS MY SEX LIFE ANY OF YOUR CONCERN?

So, I started writing story series in 2016, and my stories address sex and sexuality between singles and married folks alike, touching on issues of life that concern us all. Over time, I became even bolder about writing about sex and sexual experiences. I soon realised that some people were uncomfortable with this. Fortunately, I overcame any embarrassment I had with sex when I wrote my third series, Broken, which is now a free book. It was actually while writing it that I realised the need to address this issue of sex, sin, and shame in Christianity.

Writing these stories has been my way of trying to bring sex out of the SHAME closet, where it seems the Church has thrown it. God made sex for us. We shouldn't be embarrassed about it... We shouldn't think that it's for the world and not for us. We should be revelling in it legitimately and showing them how it's done, rather than condemning sex and 'stealing' secret pleasures.

One of my readers noticed this development and asked me about it, wondering if I was not causing people to sin by the sex scenes I illustrated in my writing. I shared my response to the reader in my blog series; **Reader Questions**. However, there was another question by a reader that shocked me more. The lady asked:

"Please I want to ask as touching this issue of erection that Ifeanyi is always having. Is it because he's emotionally attached to Amaka? Or it's a normal thing for men when they see a lady irrespective of emotional

attachment and does it mean the fact that one is a Christian, the issue of the erection can't be ruled out? Or is it because Ifeanyi lived a rough life? And probably that's his besetting sin? Ma, I used to think the emotional arousement should only be felt for your spouse. I hope I'm understood and I've not muddled up my questions. Thanks."

It makes you wonder what people are being told about sex that they would think an erection is something Christian men don't or shouldn't have, except for their wives. I replied thus:

"An erection is a normal reaction of a healthy male to sexual arousal. It is purely a sexual, and not an emotional response, and happens when he is attracted to a woman, or turned on by a woman or thoughts of a woman. Christian men also have erections, and men usually wake up with erections too. It isn't a bad thing; it is just that we need to control the outlet for such arousal."

I think this miseducation or lack of education and appreciation of sex and sexuality among Christians have caused many to think that anything sexual is worldly or sinful. We need to redeem sex, as the holy, godly expression of love and intimacy that it is. It seems as though many people feel they can only enjoy sex when it is illegitimate, i.e. pre-marital or extra-marital affairs. To them, that's sweet sex.

Sex in marriage is seen as boring, dutiful, and habitual. It's not romantic. It's not sensual, freaky, or adventurous. The forbidden fruit is far more promising of pleasure in their eyes... But this is a deception of the enemy. To make us treat as despised what ought to be cherished. Because the devil hates legitimacy! He hates goodness and righteousness and justice. He hates marriage.

This is the Biblical counsel on sex in marriage: "*Let thy fountain be blessed: and rejoice with the wife of thy youth. Let her be as the loving hind and pleasant roe; let her breasts satisfy thee at all times; and be thou ravished always with her love*" (Prov 5:18).

It doesn't need to be bad to be sweet. When it's good, it's sweet, with no aftertaste! It's liberating and exhilarating. The

Scripture says to *always* be ravished by your spouse. Sex isn't an unholy activity that you should avoid, even if you are fasting. But if you would rather abstain from it while fasting, to keep your focus, that's just as good. But do not deny your spouse because of holiness (1 Cor 7:5). It is not holier to have sex less - it is dangerous for your union. As often as you can, come together sexually.

The challenge with sex being confined to marriage is the issue of sexual compatibility and mutual satisfaction. That is also an issue that is causing problems for many marriages, and a discourse on sex and sexuality will not be complete without it. It is actually a very huge issue, so I think it would be best to continue with it in a separate chapter.

S for Sex and Sexuality (2)

THIS CHAPTER IS FOR THOSE WHO are married but are not sexually compatible with their spouse and want to know how to overcome this. Singles may also find it insightful.

SCENARIO ONE

So, you waited for marriage to have sex with your spouse, and it was not all you imagined nor expected it to be... Maybe you are not so compatible. It could be that one wants it more or less than the other, or he doesn't wait for you before he comes, or she takes too long to climax. Maybe it hurts during sex, or maybe the 'little man' is hard to arouse... Maybe they are not adventurous enough, or maybe they are too adventurous.

Whatever the issue may be, you were unable to factor all

this into play before you said "I do," because you chose to obey God and wait until marriage to have sex for the first time. And now you're stuck with him or her, to be content and faithful to them for the rest of your life... You may be wondering if you will ever get past this and actually start enjoying your sex life... And perhaps you worry that if they are not satisfied sexually, they will go elsewhere for relief and satisfaction.

SCENARIO TWO

Perhaps one or both of you didn't wait until marriage to have sex. Though you were not sexually active together, one or both of you might have been sexually active previously. And now, sex with your spouse is a let-down. Perhaps you have had better. Or perhaps you are not compatible in the ways already addressed in Scenario One.

However, you didn't know you were not compatible because you actually waited to marry before you had sex with each other. Now, because you have something to compare it to, it may be harder to be content with your current sex life. It may also be harder to trust your spouse to be faithful to you when you know they have been promiscuous before and are now dissatisfied sexually with you. You may worry about your own ability to meet up to their expectations, and this is probably affecting your self-esteem and ability to perform or enjoy your time together.

Scenarios one and two present real issues that I think many people face in their marriages. They need to be addressed sensitively so that the marriage union will be strong against intruders. Even if you do not worry about your spouse cheating, perhaps you are worried about your own ability to remain faithful. As you have less and less sex, due to disappointment, the lack of sexual intimacy between you may pull you apart and present opportunities for one or both of you to falter. You need to resist this.

Compatibility is not an exact science, unfortunately. You can't know who you will be sexually compatible with, especially if you have been chaste (not kissed) in courtship. It can be disheartening having to work on your sex life when you've just begun a marriage, and you expected that you would be delirious with happiness. It can also hurt your pride or self-esteem to know or think that you are unable to satisfy your mate in bed.

If you are single, you might be wondering how you can prevent yourself from experiencing such disappointment without disobeying God and 'sampling' sexually, as your mates may do and encourage you to do. **It is good for you to remain faithful to God and keep yourself for your spouse.** There are other and more important factors in play for you to enjoy a happy marriage. If you are following God, He will lead you to the right person, with whom you should share, not only spiritual and emotional compatibility but also, sexual compatibility.

Remember, marriage is more than sex, so do not, for fear of sexual incompatibility, sabotage your union by disobeying God. Trust Him. His way is best.

If you are struggling with sexual compatibility in your marriage, there are a number of things you should do to resolve this.

> **1. Admit it to yourself.** Before you can solve any problem, you have to admit that there is a problem to solve. Denial will not make the problem go away. Fear of confrontation will not resolve the issue either. The truth will set you free, so admit it, and then pray for God to help you to work it out and bless your marriage with sexual compatibility;
>
> **2. Bring it up sensitively with your mate.** Now you have admitted it to yourself, it's time to do something about it. It begins with you being honest with your

spouse. They may not actually know that you are unfulfilled sexually. They may be trying hard to please you and not even know that all their dramatics is a turn off... The problem might be easily resolved with an honest but sensitive confrontation that is not accusatory. Perhaps you can start by asking them about their sexual satisfaction rather than telling them outright that you are unhappy. Then after they have answered (hopefully, they will be honest and not try to say what they think you want to hear), you can now say how you feel while appreciating the efforts they make to please you.

3. Talk about sex and what pleases you openly. Now that it is out in the open that you have an 'issue,' it is time to talk honestly about how you can work on it together. Sexual compatibility is not ONE person's fault or problem. It is a shared problem, and unless it is a biological factor (e.g. erectile dysfunction), the fault lies with both of you - if you must lay blame.

It is good to start with the positives before going into the negatives. Maybe s/he is a good kisser. Maybe you appreciate the time they take in foreplay. Maybe you like the way they look into your eyes and call your name or pet name. Talk about what you appreciate, then you can talk about what you would like MORE of. As much as you can, be positive in your approach. Nothing inspires more than praise. Finally, you can talk about what you would like less of. Also ask them, and listen to their criticisms or perspective. Most of all, try not to take offense. It is not a competition nor a personal attack. You're a unit, and if you get it right, you'll soon be singing each other's praises... So, work together.

4. Make more effort and time to be intimate with each other sexually. Now that you have confronted the elephant in the room, don't leave it there. You need to actively work on getting it out. Don't be discouraged by the feedback you received. Take everything to God in prayer. Pay more attention to your spouse and look for opportunities for you to put to practice the things you discussed. Experiment with positions. You can introduce chocolate or mousse or other foods that might help in foreplay. Take note of what works and what excites your spouse and build on that knowledge. Don't be shy to guide your spouse when in bed together, but try not to be bossy (unless they say they like it). Afterwards, you should talk about how it went. Try to be romantic and playful with it, not like you are marking him or her after a test. Spend time cuddling after. **The trick is to DEVELOP intimacy, rather than trying to be skilful sexually. Intimacy changes everything because great sex is more a mental and emotional accomplishment than it is physical.**

5. Practice other forms of intimacy to stimulate you towards sexual intimacy (Read I for Intimacy). Foreplay is not limited to sex time. Foreplay should start well before you get to the bedroom by the intimacy you show each other. You can touch and kiss often. Talk sweetly to each other. Or dirty... Dress sexy and tease each other. Spend time with each other doing other things besides sex, which will increase your general intimacy. And then, when you get to the bedroom, invest in some more foreplay time. Try not to rush into penetration so that the wife is well NATURALLY lubricated and more likely to enjoy sex too. And of course, the wife needs to stimulate her husband so that he remains hard (if that is a challenge).

6. Consider professional or medical consultation and treatment. If things don't seem to be improving, or the pace seems painfully slow, it could be time to get some external assistance. You need to be sensitive about bringing this up with your spouse because of bruised egos. Low self-esteem is a killer to a happy sex-life. However, when you are desperate, you've got to do what desperate people do and get help before it is too late! Do some research and bring your findings to your spouse. Discuss the options together. If there is a pill you can take to improve your performance, don't be too proud to do so. If you need a lubricant to get things going, don't be too shy about adding this either. It's probably best to try some natural remedies before going for drugs. It may be that, as your self-esteem improves from past successful sessions, you will actually lose your reliance on these things that aided you to get your first or previous orgasm/s. A professional will be able to guide you better, so seek professional advice.

7. Look after yourself, and make yourself more attractive to your mate. Don't stop looking after yourself or trying to look appealing to your spouse. If they are being negative, pray for them and encourage them to persist in working on it together. Eat healthy. Work out. Dress attractively. Groom yourself. Let them know that you are still and always available sexually. Sometimes, these things that we do to make ourselves more attractive to the opposite sex also make us hornier (as we begin to feel sexy). So, if the problem is that you desire sex less than your spouse, then make more effort in this area. When you start to feel and think you are sexy, you will be horny for sex. Sometimes, the problem is just in the mind.

8. Lower your expectations. It can be hard when your expectations keep getting dashed. It could be that your expectations are too high or unrealistic. Especially if you have experimented sexually before marriage. It may help to lower your expectations to something more attainable. Maybe you can manage with sex three times instead of five times a week. Maybe if you are not able to climax with penile penetration all the time, you can substitute for his finger now and then. The point is to lower your expectations so that you can get more positive results, then you can hopefully bring them up again. The point is not to become defeated and give up. Where there is a will, there is a way, so keep trying.

9. Appreciate your time together sexually. Even if you don't come all the time, or most of the time, appreciate your sexual intimacy. It is common for men to come every time while women may not always climax during sex. Be happy for him, and don't dampen his climax by grumbling. Appreciate the time you spend touching and kissing and fondling, and keep doing those things. Do not begin to despair and distance yourself. You've got a lot more going for you than sex and orgasms.

10. Persist in your efforts, and keep praying. You can see it this way; if you give up, that's it. You lose. You both lose, and you resign yourself to being miserable. The only way to win is to keep trying. You can take a break from the pressure for a while, but don't let it be too long. Talk to God about it, and build your faith in Him. Keep being kind and affectionate with your spouse, and keep making yourself available. Keep working on your intimacy. With genuine love, true intimacy, persistence, professional help, and prayer, you can't lose. Trust God!

You are the one in the marriage, and only you know how bad your situation is. I hope my advice will help you, and if you feel you need professional intervention, don't be shy to seek such help. It is worth it to have a happy sex life. But what you don't want to do is lose your faith in the process…

Whatever happens, your faith is your greatest treasure, so

don't give up your faith in God, and don't step out on your marriage. That won't help anybody. It will only make a hard situation harder or even impossible.

As tough as it may be, you may need to prepare yourself for getting by or managing your sexual incompatibility. There are worse things that have happened to couples. You signed up for better or for worse. All I can say is remain hopeful that it will get better, and keep up your spiritual, emotional, intellectual, and physical intimacy. It will get better as your intimacy grows.

For the singles. Again, I would say WAIT on the Lord. Don't sample. You could have great sexual compatibility with someone who doesn't fear the Lord and have a horrendous marriage! But even if you do find that you need to work on your sexual compatibility, it can also be exciting discovering your sexuality with your spouse. You will be teaching and learning from each other, growing together, and thrilling each other as you become more sexually in tune. It does happen. And it will be worth the wait.

T for Temptation

DO YOU KNOW WHAT IS THE MOST common thing in the world? Temptation. Do you know what is the most NORMAL thing in the world? Temptation! Temptation is everywhere, no matter the size of the sin. Whether it is the temptation to conceal something that should be revealed, or the temptation to tell a small white lie or to concoct an exaggerated or elaborate deceptive account.

Temptation is something every mature person should be used to experiencing and overcoming. You will keep experiencing temptation because the Devil doesn't quit. And you should keep overcoming temptation because you are NOT IGNORANT of his devices... Temptation is not something you should be worried about. Foolishness is. Facing temptation is not a sin. Falling for it, which is foolishness, is!

The fool doesn't learn from past mistakes. Tempt them with the same thing a thousand times, they will fall one thousand times. The more you give in to temptation, the stronger its hold on you. It can become crippling and addictive, and you can feel powerless over it. But temptation can be overcome - no matter how long you've been a fool for it.

Temptation begins to lose its power the FIRST time you say "No" to it. It is a bit like fear... Once you face it and stand up to it and kick it out, it is harder for it to affect you again. Sure, there will still be situations where your courage and faith will be tested, but because you have defeated it once, you are bolder and SMARTER to withstand it. So, the key to defeating temptation is to become bold and wise about saying NO to it - consistently!

Temptation usually starts small. Very tiny even. It likes to creep in, and make room for itself in your life. You have to be diligent about shutting out every avenue to temptation. As well as shutting it out, you also need to insulate your life against it with wisdom. Build up your walls and tower against it so that, big or small, temptation can't do its destructive work.

The foolish think temptation is BIG, so they never cover their gaps. They are continually exposed to temptation and giving in to small doses of it that, when the big one comes, they are powerless to rebuke it, not to mention deal with it.

There are FIVE things you need to know about temptation:

> **1. It is not NEW.** There is really nothing new under the Sun (Eccl 1:9), and temptation is as old as time. Think about Adam and Eve.

> **2. It is extremely common.** It is indeed rife because we live in a fallen world, which is dominated by evil. No matter how much we avoid temptation, we will still confront it in our lives. We should not be surprised by it

or think that it is a judgement on our spirituality. Remember, even Jesus was tempted. However, we must look to God for a way out (1 Cor 10:13).

3. It starts small. Temptation is not fond of announcing itself. It wants to be received, so it will come in a way that it can be more readily accepted. You have to be very discerning and scrupulous in weeding it out of your life. Do not be careless and give the devil a foothold (Eph 4:27).

4. It can be overcome. For every problem, there is a solution. Temptation is from the devil, and the empowerment to overcome it must come from God. Do not rely on your own strength, but seek God's face when tempted and ask for the grace and wisdom to overcome (Jam 1:5, Phil 4:13).

5. Persistence is the key to overcoming. You only lose once...and that's when you give up the fight. As long as you're in the race, you are winning, no matter how often you fall. Your falls are only occasions to learn how you can perfect your strategy, and also so you can help others not to fall but to win. So, do not give up, do not tire of resisting evil, and keep choosing life (Gal 6:9).

Here are FIVE things you need to do to overcome temptation:

1. You must be able to recognise it. *This requires discernment.* You need to know the truth, so that you can be able to identify a lie and not fall for it;

2. You must acknowledge it. *This requires honesty.* If you live in denial, you are already falling for temptation;

3. You must pray about it. *This requires humility.* You can't fight this battle in your own strength, and you need to be humble and confess that you need God;

4. You must flee and shut it out. *This requires sincerity.* You need a love for the truth, so you won't compromise for evil. Don't give it a chance to explain, advertise itself, or otherwise persuade you;

5. You must nourish yourself with wisdom. *This requires fellowship with God.* Spend time studying the Scriptures and communing with God in prayer. Build up your fortress again, and abide in Christ, so you are less likely to face temptation and more able to respond in wisdom when confronted by it, like Jesus did.

If you have fallen into temptation, despite fleeing or resisting it, you should:

1. Confess your fault. Humble yourself. You are not the first to fall, and you won't be the last. Yes, you thought you were better than that, but dwelling in pride won't undo what has been done. Admit your error, so you can be cleaned and restored.

2. Forgive yourself. It can be hard realising the damage you have caused and living with it. But dwelling on the past won't help you in your present or future. Learn from it, move on, and use it as an opportunity to help others.

3. Receive forgiveness from those you offended and God. Believe that God has forgiven you, that He has separated your sins from you as far as the East is from the West (Psa 103.12). Understand that it may be hard for others to forgive, but when they express their forgiveness, accept it and appreciate them for it.

4. Fix the damage. This can be hard, but it is very important for healing that you do what is needful to restore trust into your relationships, after sin has breached it. You will need to remain humble, and keep owning your fault without condemning yourself. What is needed is love because love covers a multitude of sins (1 Pet 4:8). So, practice sincere love.

5. Rebuild your fortress against further temptation. Don't be afraid to start building again, even from the foundation. Lay a good foundation and strong walls, by having fellowship with God and other believers and doing what will strengthen your personal faith and your relationships.

Let's connect this with marriage. When people think about temptation in marriage, they usually think about sexual temptation and infidelity. It is probably because it is the BIGGEST and most common form. It is very important to "affair-proof" your marriage, by building up your fortress and air-tight shutting all avenues to sexual temptation.

These FIVE steps should serve as a guide:

1. Choose your friends wisely. Friends influence what we do and say and who we become. The wrong sort of friends can become weeds in a marriage garden, choking out the trust and intimacy between the couple. The right sort of friends enhances the marriage with godly counsel and support;

2. Set and keep boundaries on intimacy, emotional as well as physical, with others besides your spouse. You need to be careful about the signals you are sending to those outside your relationship. If you are overly intimate with others, you might be communicating that your needs are not being met at home, such that there is room for them to come in. If you need more intimacy, let your spouse be your first resource. This also makes your spouse feel safe and protected.

3. Immediately end, without need of an explanation, any relationship that is compromising on your

boundaries or where you feel unduly attracted to the person. This is extremely important. Anyone who is seeking a competing position in your life to your spouse is an ENEMY of your marriage, the same way anyone/thing seeking a competing position to God as the lord of your life is an enemy of your faith. You must resist them and, ultimately, run from such. Don't worry so much about other people's feelings. The person whose feelings you ought to protect is your spouse, and you need to ensure that they know that they come second only to God.

4. Surround yourself with people who believe in your marriage, support you and your spouse, and who share your values in life. Iron sharpens iron (Prov 27:17). Such relationships will give you a rich perspective on what marriage is and can be and encourage you to persevere towards it. If ever one of you falls, they will be there to help you both get on your feet and will not be like vultures, looking to swoop in and take advantage of your weakness.

5. Grow your intimacy with your spouse and with God. Read I for Intimacy to learn more about how to improve intimacy in your marriage. Read my blog post, **Conversations with God,** to learn about how to improve your communication with God. When your connections to these two most important people in your life are strong, it is very near impossible that you will succumb to temptation, but you will be well-equipped to defeat it every time.

We need to be aware that the temptation that often destroys marriages doesn't only come in a sexual package. In fact, a lot more would have gone wrong before someone decides to cheat on their spouse. Other ways temptation can affect your marriage are:

1. The temptation to be selfish. Can you think of a few ways you give in to this type of temptation each day? When last did you do something just because your spouse liked it?

2. The temptation to be proud. When was the last time you doubted yourself in a disagreement? Do you hold bitterness against past failures of your spouse?

3. The temptation to be greedy. Are money problems crippling your marriage? Do you constantly feel discontent with what and how much you have?

4. The temptation to be lazy and complacent. Do you make the effort to spend time together? Are you both working towards a plan to better your marriage and Faith walk?

5. The temptation to be paranoid. Do you often doubt your spouse? Do you find yourself spying or snooping on them?

There are probably more. Two others that readily come to mind are the temptation to be secretive and the temptation to be impatient. These often happen because we are trying to preserve our individuality. You're married now. You can't have your cake and eat it too. We should always seek to cleave and be open to our spouse, making sure to include them in the things that affect our lives.

If we are able to resist and close off these avenues by practicing sincere love towards one another and faith in God, then we should have a turbulence-free marriage. **I hope that you have been able to see that falling into temptation is NOT INEVITABLE. Temptation is only a suggestion to do evil, but you have a good and sound mind to resist it. Use it!** Don't be foolish, and don't give place to the enemy. Kick out temptation before it becomes a trial of your faith and/or marriage!

U for Unity

THE SAYING IS TRUE, "*UNITED WE stand, divided we fall!*" (REF 41). Unity in marriage cannot be overrated. It is in fact what defines a marriage - two becoming one. Unity and marriage are, therefore, synonymous in meaning. Without unity, there is no marriage.

Marriages don't fall apart in a day but over a length of time when there has been disunity. The enemy takes advantage of this to create greater distance, distrust, and animosity between the couple. They are separated emotionally, mentally, and spiritually before there is a physical manifestation of their division. If you do not actively work at unity in your marriage, then disunity will take a hold. **So, a successful marriage requires two people who choose *daily* to 'marry' themselves, by continually cleaving to one another.**

Unity, though synonymous with marriage, doesn't happen on its own or overnight. It requires you to be intentional, persistent, and resilient against the things that cause division. Your only chance at success in marriage is for you to remain united with your spouse; to work together as a team, not in conflict nor competition, but on purpose and in unity.

Christ tells us that in marriage, the two people have become one flesh...not one spirit (Mark 10:8). If they are in Christ, they are bound by One Spirit, His Spirit, but they have also become one knit unit...a whole new stronger fabric (Eccl 4:9-12). One flesh doesn't mean you have become one *being* with your spouse, in that you are no longer different but the same. You are still different, you are still *you*, but you have been knit and bound to another being, such that *together* have become a single entity that is stronger by virtue of your union and the Holy Spirit that binds you.

For you to accept and live up to your new nature as ONE FLESH with another, you must first deny and die daily to your old nature as LONE FLESH without another. It is no longer about you (not that it ever really has been), and it isn't simply about your union either. It is about the message your union communicates to the world. It is about the image your union portrays of God's love, power, and wisdom. You cannot flourish as this new entity when you are still focused on your individuality. You must also be surrendered to God's will and control in your marriage to succeed.

So, for there to be unity in marriage, there is need for there to be:

> **1. Humility.** Both husband and wife need to be humble, by forsaking self and pride for the sake of their union. At this junction, it is not about who is in charge, because if you want to be in charge at the expense of your marriage, you may very well find yourself in charge alone. Not good! First things first, humble yourself, and let God exalt you (1 Pet 5:5-6, Jam 4:10, Matt 23:11-12).
>
> **2. Agreement.** This can't happen without communication, because you are not mind-readers. There

will be things you learnt about yourselves before you got married, which you agreed on or even disagreed on. Now that you are married, do not stop communicating and learning more about yourselves and growing in understanding and agreement. Read C for Communicate Effectively.

It may take some time for perspectives to change and align, but as you persist in communication, being already humble, you will certainly grow in understanding and agreement with each other, and your union will be strong. Ultimately, if there will be a chance for success, one of the things you should agree on early (preferably before marriage) is who should be the leader and who should be the follower. Ideally, you ought to submit to the Biblical model of the man leading and loving his wife as Christ loves and leads the Church.

3. Trust. As you grow in agreement, trust will grow and should be nurtured in your relationship. Things may happen (human failure, sin, temptation, tribulations etc) to test your trust in each other, but you need to CHOOSE to trust so that you do not give the enemy a foothold for separation (1 Pet 5:8-9, Eph 4:26-27). Pray for yourself and your spouse continually, that each of you may be strong in times of trials and temptation and gracious with each other should either falter (1 Pet 4:7-8), trusting God to work all things out for His good purpose (Rom 8:28). You should also build trust by being transparent with your spouse. Cultivate a deep intimacy in your relationship through honesty, and it will be easy to trust. Your trust to your spouse says, "I believe in you... I believe in us." It binds, it liberates, and it produces the good fruit of faithfulness.

4. Submission. This requires both trust and respect, from both partners again. Submission is the practical manifestation of humility, a spiritual condition. When you humbly submit to one another, you will not dwell on what you are giving up but what you are investing in...what you are *building* up. You do what is necessary to get the result you desire, knowing that everything can and should be forsaken for your union...including self. Read D for Die Daily to Self. Submission is, therefore, an act of love; for whatever and whomever you would submit to, you love and cherish. You submit by caring for, sharing with, and uplifting one another through continuous acts of kindness.

5. Faithfulness. Trials and temptations are TESTS. That is all they are. They are not a sentence on your marriage, but they *can* become *tools* in STRENGTHENING your marriage. Rightly handled, they can be purifiers and moulders. They are tests, which are never easy nor enjoyable, from which you will learn about yourself and your spouse, and through which you have a chance to overcome together as you learn to work as a team. Because it is not ONE person being tested, it is your UNION - your *fabric*, if you like - which you are now fully invested in. You must be faithful and be long-suffering, hanging on and continually cleaving to each other (1 Cor 13). Be faithful in humility, agreement, trust, and submission, and no matter the storm, you will overcome it together. If anyone falters, remember, all that is needed is FORGIVENESS for you to continue in your vocation of love. Don't ever think something is too much to forgive. Remember how much you have been forgiven (Luke 7:47, Matt 6:14-15).

By virtue of your marriage, you are already one fabric. But you determine the type of fabric you are by how much you cleave to each other. If you were not attracted to each other, you would not have sought to marry and then married. Now you are married, work with God and each other to stay united, by fuelling the fire of love and attraction. He is on your side to succeed. He is for unity, not division, so know that, with His help, you cannot fail!

When tough times come, when trials and temptations come, and in those odd lazy days when marriage is work or your partner is unattractive or unappealing to you, and you would just like a break from being married (if not a permanent separation), this is the time to CLEAVE even more. At these points, nature and evil are wrestling to tear apart what has been bound, and it may feel natural to give in, but you must actively resist this and choose to 'marry' your spouse again. You must choose to be married and not entertain thoughts of singleness, even for a moment.

Once you are called in marriage and bound unto another in this noble vocation, singleness is no longer your portion, nor profitable for you. To separate will be a severing of your fabric; your new self, which is now bound to your spouse. However attractive the thought of being single is; for you, it is brokenness. Get the right perspective and fight for your marriage! The odds are indeed stacked in your favour because it is God's will for you to succeed.

"What therefore God hath joined together, let not man put asunder" (Mark 10:9).

V for Victory in the Vine

"I am the vine, ye are the branches: He that abideth in me, and I in him, the same bringeth forth much fruit: for without me ye can do nothing" (John 15:5).

VICTORY IN MARRIAGE IS guaranteed when we are connected to the Vine, as branches, and we abide in Christ, who enables us to do all things (Phil 4:13). Problems arise in marriage when we try to do it in our own strength, with our own wisdom, depending on our limited and fickle love. Marriage, though of the world, requires divine empowerment to succeed. If you want to succeed, you have to submit to the divine.

Yes, you are probably thinking of many Christian marriages that have failed for one reason or the other. You will probably find that one of the reasons for this failure is that one or both partners were unchristian, even though they were Believers. They did not abide in the Vine. They did not submit in love to one another. They did not love each other like Jesus loved them and FORGIVE and restore the other with grace when they fell. They forsook each other and their covenant.

We can't control what our spouse will do in a marriage (if they will forsake the Faith or not) or how they will react to our human failure (if and when we fail to live up to our calling in Christ). We can only choose to do our part and obey, submit, love, forgive, and persevere... *Marriage calls for faithfulness, and it starts with you. You must choose to be humble, long-suffering, and gracious when you are wronged and offended, just as Christ was and is to you.*

Though it is hard to do so alone, two people giving up and being selfish and unchristian in a marriage is definite failure without revival. But if at least one abides in Christ and is dependent on Him, we call upon Him to arise on our behalf and fight with us for our marriage... And such faith always moves God to act on our behalf. This is what is required of each one of us in marriage. We are to be Christ to our spouse and love them as Christ loved and loves us. And even the worst sort of marriage can be turned around.

Do you doubt this? Do you think it is too hard? An impossible calling...? All things are truly possible with God (Matt 19:26) and for him who believes (Mark 9:23).

In 2016, I wrote a fictional story, Broken, as God led me to, about a marriage that should probably never have been and should not have survived but did...by the power of God. In this story, my character, Promise, was sexually abused as a child and became promiscuous as a teenager, and she continued in this vice into adulthood. Her husband, Ope, knowingly married her, despite her faults and her lack of belief in God, because he was being obedient to God's unique call for his life.

But in the marriage, she was unrepentantly unfaithful, and she finally did an unthinkable thing to break him so that he would let her go. And he did let her go, though he continued to pray for her and remained faithful, hoping that God would do a work in her that he could not do. By the end of the book, God did, in His own way. He intervened and restored their marriage.

It is an unbelievable story, quite like the story of a God who so loved the world that He gave His only begotten Son to redeem it (John 3:16). Many were content to know that my story was fiction and said to me that it could never happen. No man could take what Promise did to Ope. No *African* man, for that matter, would put up with half of what Ope endured with Promise. "It is unrealistic," they said... And even I was thinking, though I knew the message and power that God was communicating through the story, "*this seems impossible, Lord, and I really can't tell anyone to endure such in their marriage!*" It was enough to know God loves us that way and believe that no human ever could.

Until I met Victoria (fake name). I believe our meeting was fated, and I still thank God for that encounter. Victoria was invited to speak at a small fellowship that I had also been invited to visit and speak at (about my charity). She came with her husband of about three dozen years. The husband spoke first, and he talked about how God will use your spouse to love you. He said some of the things that God has been teaching me about marriage, which I have shared in my stories and this collection, and I was so encouraged. It was really an "Oh, my God!" moment for me.

Then his wife spoke. And she revealed that her marriage had been HELL! She had actually initially decided to leave him after the first year, and she left for her sister's place in her nightgown because she was sure she couldn't survive her husband. What was he? An unrepentant philanderer, who did not care to keep his affairs hidden! She returned to him with a push from her mother to honour her vows and a resolve to let go and let God deal with her husband.

It took them seven years! She endured this horrible husband for seven years, and she died daily to self. She loved him despite himself. She bore him children, and she prayed and hoped in God and was comforted only by God. Eventually, God brought the man to his knees when he was afflicted in his health. God broke and humbled him - she said, "*God showed him who was God!*" - and he repented of his evil ways. And he loved and cherished his wife who didn't give up on him. They now go about speaking about their marriage, and the woman boasts that she now has the best husband in the world!

Some may say this is unbelievable and inadvisable to use as a case study. But what this story did to me was to help me see that when we apply God's word with faith and put Him to the test, He will honour it. If we will not fight for our marriages, if we will not be long-suffering with our spouses, do we truly expect to experience His power in our lives?

As He said to me some time ago - **My power is in humility.** Never forget that God resists the proud and gives grace to the humble (Jam 4:6). This story is a reminder that NOTHING IS IMPOSSIBLE FOR GOD (Jer 32:17, 27), and that if we are persistent in prayer and continue to abide in Jesus, God will answer us and deliver us (Luke 18:1-8).

So, if you are going through a challenge in your marriage, and you fear that you cannot survive it, take courage! Trust in God. Victory is guaranteed in the Vine. Abide in Jesus, learn from Him...follow Him to that Cross where He died, and die too...to self, and rise up to live for Christ in your marriage.

I will leave you with these Five Steps to Victory in Marriage.

1. Choose *Virtue* and Reject *Vanity*. Okay, you really don't want to enter a marriage where you will spend the whole time fasting or on your knees praying for your spouse. You want to enjoy a sweet and peaceful marriage. Then begin by choosing wisely. Walk in virtue, and follow virtue. Do not be deceived, distracted, nor blinded by appearances (John 7:24, 1 Sam 16:7). Choose someone who is SURRENDERED to Christ, a virtuous man or woman not given to vanity, and they will love you like Christ. But if you want to be worthy of them, you ought also to be so surrendered to Christ because someone like that is not foolish... They too are looking for a mate who is wise and humble.

2. Have and Keep the *Vision*. It is true that people perish for a lack of vision (Prov 29:18, Hos 4:6). Plans fail for people who lose sight of their purpose. In order to have a chance at success, you need to know what success looks like and consider if you are willing to pay the price (Luke 14:28-33). Is what you envision worth the hassle and sacrifice of self in marriage? Is success about having a house with three kids and a husband or wife? Or is success about being in a loving relationship where you are valued and are able to live up to your godly potential? Do you have the same vision for what success looks like? Is Christ at the centre of that vision?

3. *Value* Your Relationship. Cherish your spouse, as yourself (Gal 5:14, Matt 7:12). You are now one, and your fate is tied, as Fortune Friends. Your victory in marriage is dependent on the value you place in this relationship. You've got to appreciate each other and what you individually bring to the relationship. You ought to hold each other with the highest honour (second only to God). Do not treat yourselves with contempt, and be gracious and quick to forgive wrong so that your relationship, which you value, is preserved though tried by fire.

4. Be *Vigilant.* "*It is impossible but that offences will come...*" (Luke 17:1). Offences will definitely come, and the enemy will try to scatter what the Lord has joined. But you don't need to help him by being complacent or even being a tool of destruction in your own marriage. Be watchful, and resist the enemy (Matt 26:41, Jam 4:7). Be vigilant about the condition of your mind, heart, body, and spirit (Prov 4:23). Take heed of yourself, lest you fall (1 Cor 10:12-13). Do not give place to the enemy by remaining angry, refusing to forgive, or even prolonged separation (Eph 4:26-27, 2 Cor 2:10-11, 1 Cor 7:5). He is indeed a roaring lion, seeking whom he will devour (1 Pet 5:8). Act with wisdom, and you will save yourself many troubles and put the enemy to shame.

5. Remember Your Vows. When we signed up for marriage, we affirmed that we would give *unconditional* love to our spouse; "*for better or worse, richer or poorer, till death separates us.*" We made a lifelong commitment and entered a covenant with another, which was sealed by God. This commitment will be tested, and there will be many times that we will want to renege on it. But it helps to remember this solemn promise we made when we were much happier, and why. The promise was made because we KNEW hard times would come to test our resolve, so if we go back on the promise during such times, then we make the promise a *lie.* These are the times that the vow was made for. It was a confession that when challenges come, we will stick it out. And as we remember this confession, it will strengthen our resolve and help us see that the situation we are facing can be overcome, and we should not to give up nor break covenant but be reliable people of integrity.

Jesus actually said we ought not to make vows, promises, nor pledges, by swearing oaths. Swearing oaths undermine our integrity and give the impression that our word is not enough, that we are not honest people. So, Jesus said, "*let your 'Yes' be 'Yes,' and your 'No,' 'No.' For whatever is more than these is from the evil one*" (Matt 5:37, NKJV). We should be people of our word, who need only to live honourably...and faithfully.

When we make commitments, we should keep them. As with all things, we must be reliant on God's grace to enable us to be obedient, even in this regard. As long as we abide in Christ, we can be people of integrity, whose 'yes' means 'yes' and 'no' means 'no.' And if we are faithful, God will show Himself faithful in our lives, and no matter the storms we face, we can declare that "*...we are more than conquerors through him who loved us*" (Rom 8:37).

AUTHOR'S NOTE

I wrote this chapter almost four and a half years ago, and every time I thought of publishing The Marriage ABCs, I felt it was a chapter I might need to change or remove altogether. Not because it is no longer true, but because it seems so unreasonable to expect someone to put up with such wickedness in order to fulfil all righteousness.

Since I wrote it, I've written more novels, **Perfect Love** being one. Perfect Love was about two people who did not love each other anymore and who were flirting with temptation. But with their reconnection to the Vine, they pulled through. As powerful as it was, I was not satisfied with this story, because it isn't the reality for many. I decided to explore another angle...

I wrote **The Naïve Wife Trilogy**, which is about a woman deceived into marriage by a fraudster. And this guy had no plans on changing, though, like a chameleon, he maintained appearances for a long time, and his wife struggled to understand him and what was happening in her marriage. She abided with him, hanging on to this very teaching to the point of endangering herself.

I had to ask God…is this really the only way for your daughters to gain victory? By exposing themselves to sexually transmitted diseases, financial abuse, emotional abuse and neglect, while their children watch them suffering (**please skip ahead to the last chapter if your case involves violence, physical or sexual**)? Where is Your justice? Your deliverance?

As I wrote the story, I really didn't know where it would lead. I only knew the husband was not going to change, so what was God going to do about that?! Well, the final part of the trilogy is out now, with the release of this book, so you can read it and see what happened.

But I just wanted to say, I know this chapter is hard. However, the truth is still the truth. THERE IS NOTHING IMPOSSIBLE FOR GOD TO DO. And I would never encourage anyone to give up on their marriage or to sin. But if you do give up, I can understand and will not judge you. There is grace enough for our healing and restoration. We are not perfect. But God is able to make us perfect, and we are still on this journey with Him.

Some people may have testimonies like Victoria, and others will talk about how they escaped with barely the clothes on their back… Unfortunately, some may not survive it or leave with a sexual disease or a mental health condition! Let each person do according to their faith. May God help you and bless you.

Love, Ufuomaee.

W for Wisdom is the Principal Thing

EVERYTHING ABOUT MARRIAGE IS WISDOM. Marriage is an expression of God's Wisdom and Love (Eph 5:22-33). As such, it is holy. It is sacred.

"Marriage is honourable in all, and the bed undefiled: but whoremongers and adulterers God will judge" (Heb 13:4).

The idea of marriage is wisdom. The design and practice of marriage is wisdom. The success and beauty of marriage is wisdom. Marriages fail at the introduction of foolishness, and the prevalence of it!

We ought to think carefully and soberly when considering

marriage. It is not for fools. If you enter it foolishly, it will not bear the good fruit of love, joy, and peace that it ought to. It will be a stronghold, a burden, a cross for you that will break you and require your absolute surrender to the Wisdom of God to overcome and, ultimately, turn it around. But fools don't have such patience. They dash in and dash out of marriages, never understanding its true purpose in glorifying God and moulding each partner into His image of love.

So, let us consider the wisdom in the idea of marriage:

1. It is not good for man to be alone (Gen 2:18). God identified the need for companionship, for fellowship, that man has. Not only with a woman, but with others of his kind. We were made for family and community, not for isolation.

2. Two are better than one (Eccl 4:9-12). The writer of Ecclesiastes explains the importance of friendship. More than companionship, a friend is someone you love and trust, who will stand with you, even though others walk away or even oppose you. There is a friend that sticks closer than a brother, and that is your spouse (Prov 18:24).

3. It is better to marry than to burn (1 Cor 7:9). God gave man sexual desire, and it has the function of expressing love and intimacy and also of replenishing the Earth. Marriage is the safest place for the release of emotional and sexual passions. In marriage, both parties are honoured and protected and free to enjoy sexual intimacy. Outside of marriage, such breeds confusion and distress.

4. Each man should have his own wife (1 Cor 7:2). If each person has their own spouse, there should be no sexual immorality (Prov 5:15-20). There will be peace and not chaos (Jam 4:1).

5. Replenish the Earth (Gen 1:28). Marriage is an essential instrument to the accomplishment of this command. As man and women pair up and have children, they too will pair up with the opposite sex and have more children. And the marriage covenant holds not only the couple but the family together.

Let us now consider the wisdom in the design of marriage:

1. Leave mother and father (Gen 2:24). This signifies independence. The creation of a new unit that can also bear more units. Multiplicity and passing on of heritage;

2. Cleave to your wife (Gen 2:24). Unite and bond with your spouse. This makes you a strong and powerful unit, as we saw in U for Unity.

3. Wives submit to your husbands (Eph 5:22; Col 3:18). This is orderly, for in every team that means to succeed, there must be a leader, and wives were made to honour and complement their husbands in this way (Gen 2:18).

4. Husbands love your wives as your own bodies (Eph 5:25; Col 2:19). Loving submission is the duty of every leader in the Kingdom of God (Matt 23:11). More than loving their wives as themselves, which is the sum of the Law and the Prophets (Gal 5:14), they are to love their wives as Jesus loves the Church (Eph 5:25). This gracious, passionate love provides safety for fearless, reciprocal love from their wife, who is called to obey.

5. Children are a reward (Psa 127:3). Marriage provides an ideal environment to bring up happy, well-rounded children. They are one of the fruits of a blessed marriage.

Finally, let us consider the wisdom in the success of marriage:

1. Unity. Two shall become one (Gen 2:24; Mark 10:8). It is a beautiful thing to see two people coming together in mutual love and submission. The process of becoming one transforms the two into better versions of themselves, as they grow in understanding and graciousness. Where there is unity and agreement, there is joy!

2. Sacrifice. Marriage is not simply a calling to enjoy love but to give love and practice forgiveness towards another until death separates you. It is a call to sacrificial, unconditional love that requires the greatest humility and graciousness to succeed. Love covers a multitude of sins (1 Pet 4:8) and it never fails (1 Cor 13:8). When you are protected by such absolute and unconditional love, you can truly rise to your godly potential to give true love in return because you are not afraid (1 John 4:19). Perfect love casts out all fear (1 John 4:18).

3. Harmony. Christian marriage, that is marriage entered into with Wisdom, depicts the love between Christ and the Church (Eph 5:32). It is a harmonious relationship between the two sexes; a man and a woman, a leader and a follower. It is characterised by mutual submission and respect. It bears the fruit of peace.

4. Favour. He is blessed (Prov 18:22). She is blessed (Prov 31:28). The children are blessed (Exo 20:12). A successful marriage is also a blessing to their community and society at large.

5. Legacy. Children are as arrows; they add wealth and strength to the family (Psa 127:4-5). The continuance of wisdom by training children is a treasure to the child and benefit to the world for many generations (Prov 22:6).

Though marriage is sacred, it is still of the world (Luke 20:34-36). Marriages are until death do you part, not for eternity (1 Cor 7:39). Marriage was made for Man, not Man for marriage. As such, it serves Man and not the other way round. It is good to remember this piece of wisdom and that we are called to peace and liberty, whether in marriage or not (1 Cor 7:15). Marriage is not meant to be a yoke of bondage.

This world is passing away, and the end is nigh. Christians are called to desire a holy dwelling, to set their eyes on Heaven and Eternity. Biblical teaching is that, in this world, given the foolishness and depravity of man, it is better not to marry. But it is better to marry than to burn with lust. Those desiring marriage must be sober about what marriage REQUIRES (humility) and DEMANDS (holiness).

Too often, marriage is pitched to every and anyone, and the counsel given for those seeking to enter marriage is hardly sober nor holy. It is often very worldly. There is an assumption that everyone will get married or will fornicate if they do not. Christian practice is that marriage is a choice, and not everyone made that choice in times past...and that was because they appreciated the high calling of marriage.

"His disciples say unto him, If the case of the man be so with his wife, it is not good to marry. But he said unto them, all men cannot receive this saying, save they to whom it is given. For there are some eunuchs, which were so born from their mother's womb: and there are some eunuchs, which were made eunuchs of men: and there be eunuchs, which have made themselves eunuchs for the kingdom of heaven's sake. He that is able to receive it, let him receive it" (Matt 19:10-12).

The message is clear. If you can be single, it is better to be so (1 Cor 7:8). But if you cannot, because of passion, then soberly and humbly consider marriage. Make sure that your partner is also of the Faith (2 Cor 6:14), and not a fool, so that both of you can honour it with holiness. Do not EVER, because of passion, rush into marriage! That is foolishness. Marriage and foolishness do not agree.

"Wisdom is the principal thing; therefore get wisdom: and with all thy

getting get understanding" (Prov 4:7).

X for Xclusive

IF YOU'RE IN A POLYGAMOUS marriage, you might want to skip this chapter. Some of the things written may be challenging for you to read. It isn't my intention to offend but to teach as many as are willing to take heed the way of love, truth, and righteousness.

I want to take a guess and say no one enters marriage believing and hoping that they will be one of two or more loves of their beloved's life. They enter marriage believing and hoping for exclusivity. That they will be the one and only love of their beloved's life. The last one, if not the first one.

Marriage was made for exclusivity. A man and a woman. Not a man and two or more women, nor a woman and two or more men. That is why the knowledge that the one you treated as your one and only has betrayed your confidence by cheating on you, and not considered you worthy of the same honour, is heart-wrenching! It is devastating.

Even for those few who thought they didn't mind being one of many before they got married. They will soon realise that reality bites, and that was not EVER their heart's desire...to share their beloved with another. It was a compromised choice, during a period of lowered self-confidence and esteem, when they despaired of love or losing their beloved.

Knowing that you wouldn't want to be so treated, to be among one of many wives or husbands or to be cheated on by your spouse, you ought not to treat them so. Do unto others as you would have them do to you (Matt 7:12). Give the kind of love that you expect to receive. And if you know you are too selfish to be exclusive, then deny them the rights of marriage...for marriage was made for exclusivity (Heb 13:4).

When two become one, another one cannot be bound to the two and they will still remain one! For another to be bound, the two must first be severed. And if they are severed to make inclusion for another, they cannot be bound together the same way, and the third addition will never result in the three becoming one again. They are no longer one. They are three entities, which are broken and compromised. There is no unity. But most of all, God is absent from such unions.

So, you heard of polygamous unions that the Lord blessed. You're probably thinking of the story of Jacob and Leah and Rachel as recorded in Genesis 29. Do you think such happened or was written as a 'good' example to us? No, it was simply an account of what happened in the past (an historical account of the lineage of the Jews), not an inspirational story to give us lessons on marriage. But we can certainly learn from it...as we do all Scripture (2 Tim 3:16-17).

Did Jacob marry both Leah and Rachel in obedience to God or to fulfil his desire to marry Rachel? Do you think Leah was happy in that marriage? Do you think Rachel was? Did you not read of the endless competition between the sisters and the strife and division among their children?

God commanded the Israelites not to sleep with two

siblings (Lev 18:18), so Jacob marrying Leah and Rachel, even though it was before the Law was passed, was still contrary to God's will and Spirit. Leah was despised by Jacob, so God had mercy on her by opening her womb, and He humbled Rachel, whom Jacob loved. Was Jacob at fault for marrying Leah in the first place?

Yes, I believe he had some blame in the whole ordeal, but mostly, he was tricked by Laban, who did this wickedness to his daughters for whatever reason. But out of this situation, God brought out good, as He is able to do, but we ought not to test Him by entering such marriages and thinking that He will bless our union.

Polygamy hurts. Where it is the man who married more than one wife, it hurts the wives and the children and even the husband. And in the rare cases that it is a polygamous woman, it hurts the husbands and the children and even the wife. Polygamy is a selfish and unwise choice that leaves hidden pains in the lives of those hurt by it.

There will be low self-esteem, constant strife, identity crisis, lack of brotherly affection, lack of intimacy between spouses, and more. Not to mention the message that is passed on to the children about men and women's rights and duties in marriage. It is hardly an ideal environment for raising children with good values, who have respect for the equality of men and women.

Polygamy is not for Christians. Once you are married, the introduction of another into the marriage is adulterous. It is not legitimate. We know already that marriage is sacred, and when we consider entering it, we must consider wisdom. **We are not like the world, who enter marriages to satisfy their passions. We enter marriage to glorify God, having first forsaken it with all things when we came to the Cross (Luke 14:16).** Marriage is not our right! It is a privilege and a blessed calling into ministry, where the first and primary recipients are our spouse and children.

Polygamy is lustful and greedy and a great wickedness. Because it was done in the past, or because people do it today, and they seem to be managing or doing well, doesn't make it a right thing to do. It is not possible to love two people with equal passion, unless the passion that you love them with is already compromised in intensity. A spouse needs to be loved with the mutual intensity that they love, and it is impossible for a man or woman to satisfy this need for two or more people in a marriage. There will be favouritism, and *all* their wives or husbands will be short-changed.

Only God can satisfy everyone's need for love - equally and intensely. Do not attempt to do what only God can do nor believe the professions of a man or woman promising to achieve this feat. They are lying to themselves and you. Don't be deceived.

If you are already in a polygamous marriage/relationship, please feel free to disregard this chapter. I have no counsel for you. I only pray that the Lord will be merciful to you and your family.

I am writing to deter others from entering such compromised relationships so that they can have successful marriages that glorify God. I also hope that this will dissuade any selfish dreamers contemplating polygamy while already bound in marriage. If you have the fear of God at all, you will repent of this wicked thought of your heart and, instead, seek how you can better serve and love your spouse.

Y for Yield to Love

LOVE IS TRICKY BUSINESS. The advice on falling in love and staying in love seems so contrary. There are so many pitfalls in this, and no matter how hard you try to avoid it, someone always gets hurt. Most are just happy not to be the one who does; the loser. But if a relationship fails, both are losers. And in trying not to be a loser, you show that you *are* a loser because you will never truly experience the power of love until you yield to it.

Until you surrender to it, you have never known love. And it is worth knowing love. Those who have surrendered, even though they may have been hurt, attest that it was worth letting go, not trying to protect themselves from hurt, and revelling in the magic that is love.

Real love requires real sacrifice. And the first thing to die on the altar of love is your ego. Seriously. Stop playing hard to get and just BE hard to get!

You can't do love with everyone, because it is not really love. It isn't special. It isn't deep. It is cheap and counterfeit.

So, if you really want to get deep with someone, and yield in love with another human being, then have a standard. Value yourself. Not everyone should have a chance at breaking your heart. Know your value, and go for someone who appreciates it, and who also has and knows their value.

And when you find someone who is worth it, don't be afraid to surrender to love. Quit with the games. The games are for losers. If he or she is playing games, then they are not worth it. They are not it. They are NO ONE SPECIAL.

They are not being wise, nor careful, nor taking it slow because they are nursing a broken heart. If they are still nursing a broken heart, they are not READY to consider marriage. And if marriage is not on the agenda, then what are your 'wasting' love for? How deep can you go when you are only testing the waters? Seeing where this leads...

What you are doing is satisfying your ego, feeding your flesh, appeasing your loneliness. It is selfish and wicked to engage in a relationship that calls for love and not to actually offer love. And love has wisdom. Wisdom says, "*I charge you, O daughters of Jerusalem, that ye stir not up, nor awake my love, until he please*" (Songs of Solomon 8:4). This means, don't stir up love unless you are ready for it. And again, we are warned, "*Can one go upon hot coals, and his feet not be burned?*" (Prov 6:28). This means, if you play with fire, you will be burnt.

If you do not heed wisdom, you will get burnt. You will damage yourself for love and hinder your ability to surrender to love because of fear of being burnt again. But we know that "*...there is no fear in love; but perfect love casteth out fear: because fear hath torment. He that feareth is not made perfect in love*" (1 John 4:18). **And we cannot truly walk in perfect love, until we know what it is... Perfect love was depicted on the Cross, and we are called to love that perfectly... (John 15:12-13).**

The world doesn't know love. They teach and offer a counterfeit. Their kind of love is dangerous, and it doesn't satisfy. It poses to heal, but it leaves many sick and addicted to a drug that steals their joy.

As Christians, we have and know the real thing. We have a standard, and that is Christ. And if we want to enjoy that sort of love, we have to be the sort of people that demand it, are worthy of it, and are ready to give that sort of love. And this is the love we ought to yield to:

"Love is patient, love is kind. It does not envy, it does not boast, it is not proud. It does not dishonor others, it is not self-seeking, it is not easily angered, it keeps no record of wrongs. Love does not delight in evil but rejoices with the truth. It always protects, always trusts, always hopes, always perseveres. Love never fails. But where there are prophecies, they will cease; where there are tongues, they will be stilled; where there is knowledge, it will pass away" (1 Cor 13:4-8 NIV).

If you are in Christ, you are empowered by His gracious Spirit to love like this (Phil 4:13). This is your potential in Him, to be like Him, and to show His kind of love in marriage to your spouse. Do not settle for less than this. And when you find someone special, who also knows Christ and appreciates what real love is, yield to its power... Do not be afraid.

Z for Zealous for Life

WE'VE COME FINALLY TO THE last of The Marriage ABCs. It has been rather comprehensive, with hardly a stone left unturned. I have not said much about domestic violence in marriage. It is not a part of The Marriage ABCs, because it is a given that such is contrary to Christ and to Wisdom, and thus to marriage. The Marriage ABCs has been focused on how to make your marriage better and work to the glory of God. It was written for Christians.

If you are seeking marriage, then I believe you have been equipped with wisdom to discern and choose wisely so that your marriage will be the better for it; free from strife and confusion. If you are already married, I hope that you have been encouraged and inspired to keep on persevering and to abide happily with your choice. If you are already divorced, I hope this book helped you get some perspective on what went wrong, and what you could have done differently, so that you will be the wiser for it.

One thing I need you to take away from this collection is, however wonderful marriage is, however ordained and holy your union is, marriage itself is not your purpose for living and should never become your centre. Your spouse cannot and should never become your everything - God forbid! Marriage is, and should be, one of the things in this world that *add* meaning, beauty, and joy to our lives. However, without it, we can still live full, beautiful, and impactful lives.

Life itself is the most precious gift God has given us on this side of eternity. To be alive, to be able to think and reason, to feel, to enjoy, to laugh, to breathe, to smile, to sing, to dance, and to talk...these are all pleasures we take for granted. **We were meant to enjoy life, to be fruitful, to have goals and strive to achieve them, to have family and friends, and to discover our world, appreciating all of God's creation and creatures.**

God is holy, and He wants us to be holy in *everything* we do, and that also means esteeming Him as the greatest in our hearts, minds, spirits, and bodies. So, that is why, even and *especially*, our engagement in marriage is sacred. Everything we do should be an act of worship. Singleness too is a calling. It is holy and should be done to the glory of God (1 Cor 7:17-24).

We can grow discontent with anything in this life. Anything at all. When we try to make them the centre of our existence, they will show themselves to be ill-sufficient to satisfy. It is good to know the purpose of a thing and use it within its limitations. That way, we appreciate it. We rightly use it. But when we try to use it beyond its limitations, we frustrate it. We abuse it, and it will fail us. We will fail and be bitterly discouraged and disillusioned.

Imagine trying to make a sports car fly. It was made for the road, the expressway. If we get it off the ground, it will crash! So, everything has its purpose and proper use, and God alone satisfies. He alone is the all in all (1 Cor 15:28, Col 3:11).

It is good to remember that. It is good to remember that marriage was made for Man and not the other way around. It is good to remember that there is MORE to life than marriage, than romance, than raising a family. It can be hard to imagine, especially when every song programmes your mind to expect marriage and only be content in a relationship. When everyone you meet keeps asking you if you've found him or her yet, or whether you are pregnant yet... It seems like they know something about your purpose that you don't!

Don't let this discontent or envy drive you to enter marriage restlessly...nor leave it impatiently. Paul's counsel for Believers to abide in whatever condition they were called is indeed wise (1 Cor 7:20). It is based on the realisation that marriage is nothing, singleness is nothing, only that God may be glorified in all things (verse 19 - for more on this, read my Bible study, **A HARD TEACHING**).

And for those who are not enjoying a sweet marriage... Though you have been faithful, loving, and understanding of your spouse's short-comings... Though you have prayed, sought advice and counselling, and heeded wisdom... Yet, your efforts seem to be in vain, and your partner has even taken advantage of your submissive and resilient position to push through in faith, love, and hope. If you are worn out emotionally from trying to make your marriage work...

Breathe. Just breathe. Thank God for that breath. Get some good food. Cook something delicious for yourself, and eat it. Appreciate your ability to savour food.

Get out of your house for a while. Visit friends. Or the Park. Or the Theatre. Or the Zoo. Appreciate nature and civilization.

Laugh. Smile. Cry. Write. Talk.

Help someone else in need who is suffering. Volunteer at a church, school, or charity. Do pro-bono work.

Pray. Sing. Dance.

How about starting an exercise programme? How about taking that much needed trip? Or a short and inexpensive visit to another part of your country. Or maybe going home to your town or village and catching up with family.

Listen to their stories. Hear and understand. There are a thousand and one stories similar to yours. You are not alone.

Enjoy your life. Celebrate the people that matter. Call on God as you worship Him by appreciating your precious gift of life. Tell Him you trust Him to work out the rest. Tell Him that you have no other HOPE but Him. Ask Him for direction for your life. And trust.

My dear, there is more to life! Don't let any man or woman who doesn't appreciate your gift steal your joy and deprive you of that gift. Life is really too short.

Don't stop loving them. Remain hopeful. Remain faithful, but enjoy your life. Don't lose your passion for living.

And one day, they might see you and wonder why you are so radiant. So attractive. So happy. So wise. So peaceful. Of their own volition, they will come to you. And if they do not, it's their loss.

Remember, God is enough. They were extra. They were supposed to help. But God has got you, and if they will not do what they were called to do, what they promised to do, He will make other help available to you. His Arm is not too short. His resources are not too limited. And His grace is more than sufficient (2 Cor 12:9).

God bless you my Brothers and Sisters!

Let me pray for you...

"...that he would grant you, according to the riches of his glory, to be strengthened with might by his Spirit in the inner man; That Christ may dwell in your hearts by faith; that ye, being rooted and grounded in love, May be able to comprehend with all saints what is the breadth, and

length, and depth, and height; And to know the love of Christ, which passeth knowledge, that ye might be filled with all the fulness of God" (Eph 3:16-19).

HELP! I Married a Wolf!

"Beware of false prophets, which come to you in sheep's clothing, but inwardly they are ravening wolves. Ye shall know them by their fruits" (Matt 7:15-16).

WE HAVE THIS STARK WARNING from Jesus in Scripture, but it is baffling how few of us take heed of this. The word 'prophets' sort of throws us off to only suspect people who prophesy, or who lead churches, or who teach fellowships. We are careful to observe those and believe we can easily distinguish the false from the genuine. But few are wary of those who do not appear to be in leadership of any kind but simply profess to believe in Jesus.

We are far more forgiving of their faults and their misunderstanding of Scripture. They too are growing in the

Faith like we are. No one is perfect, we say. And the truth is, there is some insincerity in us as well. We can relate to their wilfulness, not being wholly submitted to the Spirit ourselves.

It seems like harmless Christianity until you decide to marry such a person. And unfortunately, too many Believers end up married to 'Christians' by name only. Yes, they go to church. Yes, they speak and pray in tongues. Yes, they even read their Bibles and engage in ministry. But did we forget the reference to "sheep's clothing"?

"Many will say to me in that day, Lord, Lord, have we not prophesied in thy name? and in thy name have cast out devils? and in thy name done many wonderful works? And then will I profess unto them, I never knew you: depart from me, ye that work iniquity" (Matt 7:22-23).

The truth is, anyone can pretend long enough to be something they are not. That is why Jesus said, **"Ye shall know them by their fruits."** Basically, WAIT FOR IT… WAIT FOR IT… WAIT FOR IT. Do not accept someone else's word that they are Christian. Observe their fruit.

"…he that is spiritual judgeth all things, yet he himself is judged of no man. For who hath known the mind of the Lord, that he may instruct him? But we have the mind of Christ" (1 Cor 2:15-16).

Mature Christians *know* true Christians. And immature Christians fall for wolves in sheep's clothing. They do not know how to wait and discern the fruit that someone is bearing. But those who are mature have BORNE the fruit, so they can identify and distinguish those who are bearing fruit from those who are wearing camouflage.

"Do men gather grapes of thorns, or figs of thistles? Even so every good tree bringeth forth good fruit; but a corrupt tree bringeth forth evil fruit. A good tree cannot bring forth evil fruit, neither can a corrupt tree bring forth good fruit. Every tree that bringeth not forth good fruit is hewn down, and cast into the fire. Wherefore by their fruits ye shall know them" (Matt 7:16-20).

It is bad enough to be bitten by a wolf who you thought was a Brother or Sister. But to wake up to the realisation that you married one is quite another nightmare entirely! What doesn't help is the lack of counsel on how to deal with such a situation.

I am often alarmed when I hear people's accounts of what their 'Christian' spouse is or has been doing. And I tell them, "they are NOT Christian." But they insist that they are. Because at one time in the past, this person said "the sinner's prayer." And at some point, they were really fervent in the Faith... Or they even pastor a church!

But look at the fruit, dear Sister or Brother. LOOK AT THE FRUIT! Christians, who are born of the Spirit of God MATURE in righteousness. They do not deteriorate into depravity!

"Now the works of the flesh are manifest, which are these; Adultery, fornication, uncleanness, lasciviousness, Idolatry, witchcraft, hatred, variance, emulations, wrath, strife, seditions, heresies, Envyings, murders, drunkenness, revellings, and such like: of the which I tell you before, as I have also told you in time past, that they which do such things shall not inherit the kingdom of God. But the fruit of the Spirit is love, joy, peace, longsuffering, gentleness, goodness, faith, Meekness, temperance: against such there is no law" (Gal 5:19-23).

Sure, anyone can fall. And though a righteous man falls seven times, he shall rise again (Prov 24:16). I get it, no one is perfect. But is he or she falling seven times a week? A month? A year? The *same* sin? No *growth*? Come on!

Yes, we should encourage one another to grow in the Faith. We should not treat people with needless suspicion but believe with them that they have received this LIFE TRANSFORMING and EMPOWERING Spirit to walk in righteousness. But at some point, you have to call a spade a spade, and a wolf a wolf. This is not being judgmental. It is being discerning. Not just for your sake, but for others who might fall for their deception.

The Bible tells us not to believe every spirit but to test them against the Spirit of Truth and Love (1 John 4). We are also commanded not to associate with so-called 'Believers' who live as unbelievers, practicing sexual immorality, debauchery, and all sorts (1 Cor 5:9-13). And again: *"Be not deceived: evil communications corrupt good manners. Awake to righteousness, and sin not; for some have not the knowledge of God: I speak this to your shame"* (1 Cor 15:33-34).

So, clearly, we have to be able to judge for ourselves what is right and in keeping with godliness and not be swayed by people's best intentions of faith. Because guess what, *"the road to hell is paved with good intentions"* (REF 4m). Narrow is the way to Heaven, and WIDE is the road to Hell (Matt 7:13-14).

"...why call ye me, Lord, Lord, and do not the things which I say?" (Luke 6:46).

It is not all who call Jesus "Lord, Lord" who are saved and truly know Him (Matt 7:21). It is those who do the will of the Father. So, please, the first step in knowing how to deal with this problem is recognising that THERE IS A PROBLEM. You didn't marry a Christian; you married a wolf in sheep's clothing.

It could also be that you are not Christian yourself. Apply the same test of fruit in your life. Are you maturing in love?

Jesus said, *"every tree that doesn't bear fruit will be cut down"* (Matt 7:19). And again, *"...if a man abide not in me, he is cast forth as a branch, and is withered; and men gather them, and cast them into the fire, and they are burned"* (John 15:6). That is some hard teaching. Contrary to the demonic doctrine of "once saved, always saved."

"Nevertheless the foundation of God standeth sure, having this seal, The Lord knoweth them that are his. And, let everyone that nameth the name of Christ depart from iniquity" (2 Tim 2:19).

Are you still needy for milk when you should be eating strong meat (Heb 5:12-14)? Are you given to the same sins over and over? Because the Scriptures also tells us that those who are born of God's Spirit cannot continue in sin (1 John 3:9). So, Paul tells us to do a self-examination to see if we are really in the Faith (2 Cor 13:5).

The truth is many Christians marry while they are immature in the Faith and are not yet trained in discernment. The pressure to marry is so strong that many are pushed to marry, even by their pastors who should know better. Many, even in the same church, are UNEQUALLY YOKED because, while some are genuine but immature, others are pretending deceivers.

People are encouraged to marry for all sorts of reasons, including, and unfortunately, to build the church numbers. Never mind if the seats are filled with the living dead! Many are not truly serious about their salvation and that of others, which is why this continues to go on.

And when the shit hits the fan, and it is evident that the wolf is acting up and showing their true colours, the situation is patched up with the false teaching that the misbehaving spouse is just a 'Believer' struggling with a 'besetting' sin, rather than a thorough appraisal of the bad fruit bearing tree. It is quickly thrown in, *"Don't judge, or else you will be judged!"* (Matt 7:1-5). Clearly, Jesus did not mean for us to throw away our discernment, seeing as He later told us (in the same chapter) that we can distinguish true believers by their fruit...

Did Jesus not also say, *"do not judge by mere appearance, but* JUDGE RIGHTEOUS JUDGMENT" (John 7:24), meaning we **should JUDGE *rightly?*** But when you accept someone's proclamation of Faith against the evidence of bad fruit and confirm that they are 'Christian,' you are making a judgment by mere appearance.

"Do ye not know that the saints shall judge the world? And if the world shall be judged by you, are ye unworthy to judge the smallest matters?

Know ye not that we shall judge angels? How much more things that pertain to this life?" (1 Cor 6:2-3).

The real problem is MANY of those who are leading churches are the wolves and wolf-breeders themselves… That's why churches are filled with immature, disobedient, and faithless 'Christians.' The students are not greater than their teachers (Luke 6:40). We must be careful, therefore, to work out our own salvation with fear and trembling (Phil 2:12) and be choosy about whose leadership and training we subject ourselves to (1 Cor 11:1).

So, you married a wolf… First of all, I'm sorry. It is a devastating realisation. Especially when you love them from your heart, and they are breaking your heart. I am so sorry.

Now, to resolve the issue, there's only one thing that is important. Are you Christian? Are you Christian *for real?* Died to self, living for Christ, good fruit-bearing Christian? Are you in the process of dying to self? Maybe you and God are still working on that, and you are drawing closer to Him, maybe as a result of the issues in your marriage?

If you answered "Yes" to being Christian or a sincere follower of Jesus Christ, then the answer to your dilemma is "the Cross." Jesus commanded us to love one another AS HE LOVED US (John 13:34-35). That is how we will be distinguished as His followers.

This is how He loved us: while we were yet unworthy, He *died* for us (Rom 5:8). So, we must do likewise to our unworthy, unchristian spouse. We must lay down our lives for them, that perhaps they can be saved and transformed by our loving witness. Read THE MARRIAGE ABCS – V FOR VICTORY IN THE VINE.

The truth is, as long as one of you is Christian in that marriage, there is hope. Even if you married a wolf, God is in control! Love truly conquers all, and if we apply the long-suffering love of God, we're promised that it will never fail (1 Cor 13:8).

If you have not been able to answer the question, feel uncertain about what you actually believe, or you know for sure that you're not a *lover* of God or Christian by anything more than a name and church association, then it's a whole different ball game. **You are free to walk away.** You cannot be constrained by the Law of Love unless you are born of the Spirit of God, which is LOVE.

If you are Christian, by the way, you wouldn't be rejoicing at that. Because love hopes all things, believes all things, endures all things (1 Cor 13:7). Love is long-suffering and gracious.

However, we know that the carnal mind cannot comprehend the things of the Spirit, nor can it be subjected to it (Rom 8:7-8, 1 Cor 2:14). **We can only give what we have, so one cannot and should not expect holiness from unbelievers. Their primary need is salvation, after which they will receive empowerment to walk in the light.**

The truth is, if LOVE is in us, our desire will be for our spouse's salvation. Our concern will be for God's will (seeing as we have died to self). And we will see our vocation in marriage as a means to minister the Gospel to our spouse.

Paul gave counsel for Believers who find themselves married to unbelievers not to seek to depart, but to abide, hoping that perhaps they will be converted by their ministration in the marriage (1 Cor 7:12-14). Read THE MARRIAGE ABCS – D FOR DIE DAILY TO SELF.

But get this, if the UNBELIEVER departs (it is an unbeliever that will seek to depart), the BELIEVER is free (1 Cor 7:15). Because we have been called to peace. Now, you can rejoice! Remember, the Bible says that God won't give you more than you can take (1 Cor 10:13).

Yes, you messed up. You didn't wait for the evidence of faith and sincere love before pledging your life to ministry to a wolf (marriage is ministry). But that's what you did. And through this awful situation, you were pruned and have grown and have borne fruit in your character. You have learnt to be long-suffering and gracious as God has been with you. You have borne your cross in marriage. But if you have occasion to be free (by the departure of your unbelieving spouse), use it (1 Cor 7:21).

However, if you are actually both Christians, and your spouse is truly just backslidden (as happens), then with your perseverance and graciousness, you can restore your spouse and your marriage. Whatever the issues in your marriage, if you are both Christians, even if you separate, if you are both still connected to the Vine, you *will* reconcile…because of the Spirit of Love which binds you. If, therefore, both of you are fighting for your marriage to work and humbling yourselves daily, you will surely overcome the challenges and enjoy a blissful marriage again.

So, the commandment for Christians in marriage is always to abide and fight for their marriage and always to work towards reconciliation (1 Cor 7:10-11).

I should point out that there is a difference between a wolf (an unbeliever masquerading as a believer) and an apostate (a former believer who has forsaken the Faith). It can be hard to tell which is which, but if they are *unbelieving,* whether they were genuine believers when you got married or were faking it, if such depart, the Believer is free. But in your liberty, do not sin (Gal 5:13, 1 Pet 2:16). Commit your ways to God, and be sure to follow His guidance on any future relationship.

Now, in the case of domestic violence, I hope no one is under any deception that the person beating his wife (or her husband) is Christian. They are at best apostate and at worst demon-possessed! Neither Paul nor Jesus gave counsel concerning domestic abuse in marriage, but we know that even in the OLD COVENANT, if a master strikes his slave (and you are not a slave), and the slave is injured, the slave GAINS THEIR FREEDOM on account of the injury (Exo 21:26-27).

Paul also tells us that if a Believer doesn't provide for his household, he has denied the Faith and is WORSE than an infidel; that is *worse* than an unbeliever (1 Tim 5:8)! It sounds like a hard judgement, but take note of this teaching. It means that basic 'care' is a kind of fruit to watch out for to know those who are truly of faith.

How then can a 'Believer' be using his wife as a punching bag or sex slave and still claim that he is interested in a marriage; that is, *loving* the woman? He has signed your freedom papers and declared that he has forsaken your marriage with his blow. You don't have to wait for such to leave, you can leave!

Please, if the man is striking you, gain your freedom! You were bought at a price, do not be slaves of men (1 Cor 7:23). To abide in such a situation is not being long-suffering, my dear. It can be very *short*-suffering and is definitely unwise. This is also not a case of turning the other cheek.

Minimally, separate, pray, and get counselling. He also needs counselling and corrective discipline. And do not be afraid to utilise the arm of the law, because the Law is for the lawless (1 Tim 1:9)! Such abusers often do not understand nor respond to compassion and grace, seeing it as weakness, but require a firm hand of authority and power to counter their oppressive spirit.

Please, **do not return** without clear guidance from God and EVIDENCE of repentance. This may take time…this is where you will need to be faithful and long-suffering. You may decide to wait, praying and believing God for their deliverance. But realise and retain the knowledge that you are not at their mercy but in God's gracious care. Abide in God and heal.

Also, you should consider the well-being and salvation of your children if you have any, and also future children if your situation is volatile. Do you want to bring or raise children in an abusive environment? Wisdom is profitable to direct.

Please ask God if you lack wisdom concerning your *unique* situation (Jam 1:5). May He help you and help us all! Amen.

Emotional Abuse
– The Silent Killer

A WORD FROM THE AUTHOR

THE IMPACT OF EMOTIONAL ABUSE on a person and their ability to function in society can be hard to determine and has largely been downplayed. But the truth is that emotional abuse is rampant. I think this is why it is hard for marriage counsellors to categorically say that it is grounds for divorce or separation.

The experience of emotional abuse is subjective, unlike physical abuse, where you can actually see the injury. The scars from emotional abuse can be buried deep, and the symptoms can be confused with other mental, spiritual, physical, or emotional ailments. It usually takes a victim who is on the verge of a breakdown, whose endurance is at its peak, to give name to the abuse they have been experiencing by speaking up. And it is even harder for them to speak up when they think that what they are going through is normal or that it would be wicked or foolish to talk about their experience and, thereby, bring their marriage and their spouse into question.

You should know that ALL abuse is emotional. If there is mental abuse, it also affects the emotions. If there is neglect, it's the emotions that take the most beating. If there is sexual or physical abuse going on, emotional abuse and manipulation would already have been firmly established in that relationship.

So, to say emotional abuse is grounds for marital separation would be saying ANY abuse is grounds for it. This could lead to a lot of marriages breaking up over petty disagreements or common issues that could normally be resolved with some counselling, patience, forgiveness, and repentance. So, how do we know when enough is enough?

For Believers, herein lies the challenge:

Love "*...bears all things, believes all things, hopes all things, endures all things. Love never fails...*" (1 Corinthians 7-8a).

As you have seen, I am a proponent of this teaching. This definition of love lays emphasis on personal sacrifice above social justice. However, this perspective makes it nearly impossible to say to a suffering sister or brother that it is okay for them to walk away from their marriage, that it could actually be the loving thing to do - to leave their spouse to bear the consequence of their constant abuse. Maybe if they suffered loss, they would realise their mistake and repent.

But you know what? I don't think Paul wrote this to encourage Believers to endure marital abuse. Marriage is hard enough without the abuse. Same goes for love and life.

Marriage is not meant to be a death trap, a place of bondage and pain. It is a place where love is supposed to be experienced, nurtured, and thriving. It is not God's will for His redeemed children to become the slaves of men through an institution He established to bless them and teach them His love. An abuse of the covenant is a breach of the covenant.

The covenant of marriage is not broken at the point that the abused finally decides to ask for help, separation, or divorce. God knows when the covenant broke and who broke it. It is not the victim who has been trying to bear all things, hope all things, believe all things, endure all things, believing that they are doing God's will by abiding in their marriage, that breaks covenant by saying, "no more abuse." It is the abuser who, despite their spouse's service, faithfulness, appeals, chastisements, and cries, chose to show hate for love because they thought their spouse would never seek help or they would not be believed.

In the case that the abuser is the husband, they must realise that they broke the covenant, which was dependent on their commitment to love their spouse the way Christ loves His Church. They are the wicked and unfaithful servants. And though the daughters of God endure at the hands of these oppressive 'leaders' masquerading as husbands, the Lord will surely deliver them and reveal His justice.

"The Lord answered, 'Who then is the faithful and wise manager, whom the master puts in charge of his servants to give them their food allowance at the proper time? 43 It will be good for that servant whom the master finds doing so when he returns. 44 Truly I tell you, he will put him in charge of all his possessions. 45 But suppose the servant says to himself, 'My master is taking a long time in coming,' and he then begins to beat the other servants, both men and women, and to eat and drink and get drunk. 46 The master of that servant will come on a day when he does not expect him and at an hour he is not aware of. He will cut him to pieces and assign him a place with the unbelievers.

47 'The servant who knows the master's will and does not get ready or does not do what the master wants will be beaten with many blows. 48 But the one who does not know and does things deserving punishment will be beaten with few blows. From everyone who has been given much, much will be demanded; and from the one who has been entrusted with much, much more will be asked'" (Luke 12:42-48).

We need to stop undermining the experience of emotional abuse, especially in the covenant relationship called marriage. Emotional abuse has long-term impact on those who endure it. The abuser uses shame, fear, self-doubt, religious ideologies, and their spouse's insecurities against them, to make them feel like they will not be understood, listened to, or even believed. For some victims, they may feel the only escape is to take their own lives. If they do not have a supportive system outside their home, they may very well choose to. And for those who escape or leave, it can take a long time for them to be delivered of all the lies they believed about their spouse, themselves, and about life, which caused them to abide for so long.

We need to make it easier for victims to get help and harder for abusers to hide in their wickedness. These two things, the difficulty in getting support and the ease of inflicting abuse without consequence, are the reasons emotional abuse is a scourge in the lives of many Believers. The Church really needs to do something about it, but be assured that Jesus will not take it lying down. He died for them; He will not let their abusers go scot free.

To gain more insight into this issue, read my fictional story, The Naïve Wife, which captures one woman's emotional ordeal in her marriage and shows how she eventually overcame it.

May God bless you with grace and truth! Thanks for reading.

Love, Ufuomaee.

OTHER RESOURCES

I would recommend that you also read my collection of articles on **Love, Sex and Marriage**, which addresses much of these issues and provides counsel to singles especially. It also contains **A Hard Teaching**, the long Bible study I did on 1 Corinthians 7. You may also find my other collections helpful in your Christian walk.

Apart from these, my novels provide lots of lessons, which can be visualised through real-world scenes, for singles and married folks, particularly **Perfect Love**. I would also recommend my latest book series, **The Naïve Wife Trilogy**, which tells the story of a Christian woman who married a wolf in sheep's clothing.

Apart from these, you may find the following titles helpful to your Christian walk and marriage:

The Peaceful Wife by April Cassidy
Avoiding the Trap of Being Offended by Kenneth W. Hagin
The Single Issue by Al Hsu
War Room by Alex Kendrick & Stephen Kendrick, novelised by Chris Fabry.
Zara: Love and Second Chances by Olusola Oguche-Agudah
You, Me, Them by The Fertile Chick
The Last Wedding Anniversary by Abimbola Dare.

REFERENCES

All Bible references were taken from **www.blueletterbible.org**. Below are some other resources I found on the Internet via Google Search.

BOOKS

1. Gary Chapman (1992). *The Five Love Languages – How to Express Heartfelt Commitment to Your Mate.* Northfield Publishing. ISBN 978-1881273158.

ARTICLES

2a. Tony & Alisa DiLorenzo (2016). *6 Forms of Intimacy to Building A Strong Marriage.* https://oneextraordinarymarriage.com/6-forms-of-intimacy-to-building-a-strong-marriage/

2b. Rania Naim (2016) *The 7 Kinds of Love and How They Can Help You Define Yours According to the Ancient Greeks.* https://thoughtcatalog.com/rania-naim/2016/02/the-7-kinds-of-love-and-how-they-can-help-you-define-yours-according-to-the-ancient-greeks/

2c. Barry R. Leventhal, Ph.D. *Money Matters in Marriage.* http://www.crosswalk.com/family/marriage/money-matters-in-marriage-1303665.html

2d. Renee Morad (2012) *10 Money Mistakes That Can Ruin a Marriage.* https://www.moneytalksnews.com/10-money-mistakes-that-can-ruin-a-marriage/

2e. Jennifer Ryan Woods (2015) *10 Ways to Prevent Money from Ruining Your Marriage.* https://www.forbes.com/sites/jenniferwoods/2015/07/06/10-ways-to-prevent-money-from-ruining-your-marriage/?sh=7d40f59544c9

2f. Steve Siebold (2015) *More Money More Problems? Not Really!* https://www.huffpost.com/entry/more-money-more-problems-_b_6532326

DEFINITIONS

3. Define Kiss - *"touch or caress with the lips as a sign of love, sexual desire or greeting"* – Google - https://www.google.com/search?q=define+kiss

QUOTES

4a. *"if you can't change your mind, why have one?"* – Edward de Bono. https://www.brainyquote.com/quotes/edward_de_bono_377965

4b. *"…with great power comes great responsibility,"* – Peter Parker Principle. https://en.wikipedia.org/wiki/With_great_power_comes_great_responsibility

4c. *"Blood is thicker than water,"* – Unknown. https://en.wikipedia.org/wiki/Blood_is_thicker_than_water

4d. *"Honesty is the best policy,"* – Benjamin Franklin. https://www.brainyquote.com/quotes/benjamin_franklin_151625

4e. *"Honesty is the first chapter in the book of wisdom,"* – Thomas Jefferson. https://philosiblog.com/2011/10/06/honesty-is-the-first-chapter-in-the-book-of-wisdom/

4f. *"…a successful marriage requires falling in love many times, always with the same person,"* - Mignon McLaughlin. https://www.brainyquote.com/quotes/mignon_mclaughlin_106607

4g. *"Kissing is one of the best kept secrets of 'happily ever after'"* – Unknown. https://www.pinterest.ca/pin/347692033706203746/

4h. *"Prevention is better than cure,"* – Desiderius Erasmus. https://www.brainyquote.com/quotes/desiderius_erasmus_148997

4i. *"Old habits die hard,"* – Lecrae. https://www.brainyquote.com/quotes/lecrae_929472.

4j. *"The only things you can count on are chaos and each other and somehow that's okay because it's a perfect kind of beautiful chaos as you see each other more clearly and know you're right where you wanna be, lack of sleep, spit up, noise and all"* – Paula Rollo.

https://www.beautythroughimperfection.com/marriage-after-babies/

4k. "*marriage is the only school where you get the certificate before you start…*" – Selwyn. https://www.scrapbook.com/poems/doc/48085.html

4l. "*United we stand, divided we fall…*" – Unknown. https://quotes.yourdictionary.com/articles/who-said-united-we-stand-divided-we-fall.html

4m. "*The road to hell is paved with good intentions…*" – Unknown. https://www.phrases.org.uk/meanings/the-road-to-hell-is-paved-with-good-intentions.html

SONGS

5a. "*You Can Get It If You Really Want*" by Jimmy Cliff (1970), written by Jimmy Cliff. Island Music Ltd.

5b. "*The Way You Make Me Feel*" by Ronan Keating (2000), written by Bryan Adams / Phil Thornalley. Universal Music Publishing Group.

5c. "*Mo Money, Mo Problems,*" by The Notorious B.I.G (1997), written by Christopher Wallace / Sean Combs / Mason Betha / Bernard Edwards / Steve Jordan / J Phillips / Nile Gregory Rodgers. Sony/ATV Music Publishing LLC, Warner Chappell Music, Inc.

ACKNOWLEDGMENTS

I thank God, first of all, for this gift and the grace given to start and finish this special collection. While writing it, I almost gave up at different points, but God empowered me and enlightened the way for me. He deserves all the glory.

I thank Him for the people He brought into my life to inspire and complete the project, to finally publish the book and make it available to you. For Toju, my husband, I'm grateful. For those who encouraged me when I was posting these articles on my blog, reading and commenting, thank you. For my patrons who supported me believing that one day The Marriage ABCs will be a book, especially Nnamdi Bolu, thank you! For Uncle John, who read the compilation and wrote the foreword, thank you so much!

Thanks to my beta readers, Onome Bada and Esther Oke. I appreciate your feedback and suggestions. By God's grace, I will be able to do a devotional or journal for The Marriage ABCs, but for now, it's really just a book, at best a study guide.

Many, many thanks to my dad for being incredibly supportive and helping me to launch my books; The Naïve Wife Trilogy and The Marriage ABCs. Who knows if I would have had the courage to publish this book without that push? It has been a long time coming.

Thanks to my mom, Rita Emerhor, and my sisters, Rhe Iwuagwu and Jite Ogwo. Thanks for the support you've given in different ways, with your counsel and finances too. I hope I can make you proud.

To all my readers, where would I be without you? Thank you so much for patronising me and spreading the word about how much you love my books! You make me a happy author.

ABOUT THE AUTHOR

Ufuoma Emerhor-Ashogbon, popularly known as Ufuomaee, is an author of faith-based books, ranging from Christian fiction, non-fiction inspirational writings, and poetry. Her passion for telling stories began as a little girl, and she started writing high school romances and poetry as a teenager, though her works were unpublished.

Ufuomaee discovered her calling for Christian ministry in 2012, when she started her blog, Grace and Truth, writing articles that addressed common issues believers face, with particular attention given to romance and relationships. In 2016, she started writing story series on her blog, and this began her journey to becoming a self-published author of over two dozen works. Her aim in all her writing is that God may be glorified and all may be edified.

When she's not writing, Ufuomaee helps other authors edit and publish their own works through Ufuomaee Business Solutions, an online technological, creative, and administrative service provider, aiding SMEs and creatives. Through this platform, she also offers website design and management services. Ufuoma is also a humanitarian, supporting those less privileged through her charitable works at Fair Life Africa Foundation, a not-for-profit organization she co-founded in January 2011.

CONNECT WITH ME

WEBSITE: https://books.ufuomaee.org
FOLLOW ON INSTAGRAM: @ufuomaee
EMAIL: me@ufuomaee.org

Printed in Great Britain
by Amazon